Palgrave Texts in Counselling and Psychotherapy

Series Editors
David Pocock
Psychoanalytic Psychotherapist & System
Calne, Wiltshire, UK

Jeremy Woodcock
Holman's Cottage
Nailsworth, UK

This series introduces readers to the theory and practice of counselling and psychotherapy across a wide range of topical issues. Ideal for both trainees and practitioners, the books will appeal to anyone wishing to use counselling and psychotherapeutic skills and will be particularly relevant to workers in health, education, social work and related settings. The books in this series emphasise an integrative orientation weaving together a variety of models including, psychodynamic, attachment, trauma, narrative and systemic ideas. The books are written in an accessible and readable style with a focus on practice. Each text offers theoretical background and guidance for practice, with creative use of clinical examples.

Rodrigo Sanchez Escandon

Contemporary Developments in Supportive Therapy

Principles and Practice

palgrave
macmillan

Rodrigo Sanchez Escandon
Clinical Psychologist, Psychodynamic
Psychotherapy, Psychoanalyst
The Tavistock and Portman NHS Foundation
Trust and British Psychoanalytic Association
Leeds, UK

ISSN 2662-9127 ISSN 2662-9135 (electronic)
Palgrave Texts in Counselling and Psychotherapy
ISBN 978-3-031-96058-1 ISBN 978-3-031-96059-8 (eBook)
https://doi.org/10.1007/978-3-031-96059-8

Cover Credit: Sergey Ryumin

This Palgrave Macmillan imprint is published by the registered company Springer Nature Switzerland AG.
The registered company address is: Gewerbestrasse 11, 6330 Cham, Switzerland

To Ruth Morwenna and Felix Titu

Competing Interests

The author has no competing interests to declare that are relevant to the content of this manuscript.

Praise for *Contemporary Developments in Supportive Therapy*

"Rodrigo Sanchez Escandon draws on his experience in public and private health settings and the demands of organising courses in psychoanalytic institutes and in the university to provide an invaluable resource for forms of therapy that are often undervalued or dismissed. In making his arguments for the importance of supportive therapy he draws on his extensive knowledge of therapeutic interventions and the difficulties faced by practitioners and patients, especially in public health services. His book should become standard reading in teaching situations dedicated to training and to understanding the internal and external constraints of working with all patients."

—Lesley Caldwell, *Psychoanalysis Unit, UCL*

"Rodrigo Sanchez Escandon makes a case for the importance and usefulness of supportive psychotherapy for helping some patients coming to therapy. He draws on a psychodynamic orientation to show how supportive psychotherapy can effectively be used to explore the various depths of feeling states that a patient may bring and a therapist may encounter in the consulting room, and how this may also aid the therapist to maintain a good therapeutic relationship and working alliance. With an accessible style, and the use of many clinical examples, this book will be very useful for psychological practitioners and trainees alike."

—Dr Poul Rohleder, *Clinical Psychologist and Psychoanalytic Psychotherapist; Senior Member of the British Psychotherapy Foundation*

"The book "Contemporary Developments in Supportive Therapy" is a unique and generous contribution, offering comprehensive coverage of the key tenets of supportive therapy and providing a thorough examination of key psychoanalytic concepts that form the theoretical foundation for applying supportive interventions. Based on extensive research and clinical responsibility, the author provides multiple clinical scenarios through case studies and clinical examples in eight chapters, discussing various possible perspectives for addressing them. The author's commitment is an essential reading for psychoanalysts and psychotherapists in practice who seek a clear guide to the practical aspects."

—Jani Santamaría Linares, PhD, *Santamaría Psicoanálisis México A.C, Mexico*

Contents

CHAPTER 1

Introduction

Introduction

Why This Book?

For several years, I have had the privilege of supervising and teaching at various institutions, including the University of Essex, the Tavistock and Portman NHS Foundation Trust, the British Psychoanalytic Association, and the Westminster Psychotherapy Foundation, among others. Through these experiences, I have observed some recurring challenges faced by many therapists: when patients either lack sufficient emotional mindedness or are too unwell to engage with complex exploratory interventions or cognitive-behavioural therapy (CBT) exercises, or when there is a fundamental misalignment between what the patient seeks from therapy and what the therapist offers.

Often, patients are not immediately seeking self-understanding or help in modifying unhelpful thought patterns. Instead, their primary need is to be listened to, supported, and to feel better in the moment. They may not be looking for problem-solving or deep insight but rather for a space to feel heard and contained. This can create a dissonance when therapists, guided by their training and professional frameworks, focus on exploring internal conflicts through interpretations, structured CBT interventions, or other model-driven procedures. Such approaches can feel intrusive,

R. S. Escandon, *Contemporary Developments in Supportive Therapy*, Palgrave Texts in Counselling and Psychotherapy, https://doi.org/10.1007/978-3-031-96059-8_1

misaligned, or even overwhelming to the patient, leading to a sense of disconnection. In many cases, this misalignment results in early termination of therapy.

It is not that therapists fail to recognize the patient's struggle. Rather, the issue often lies in the therapist's basic assumptions. Many assume that offering insight or facilitating meaning-making will inherently bring relief, following Bion's (1962) assertion that understanding is as essential to psychological well-being as food is to the body. However, in these moments, what the patient may truly need is containment and emotional support, not interpretation or a structured framework. Compounding this challenge is the fact that patients are often unable to articulate this need clearly, leaving therapists to navigate the gap between their professional approach and the patient's unspoken expectations.

Part of the reason this dynamic persists is that the value of supportive therapy has been increasingly overlooked in recent years and sometimes looked down on. The modern emphasis on quick solutions has led to a therapeutic landscape where appreciation for a therapist sitting with the patient, both struggling to understand, has become underappreciated.

The lack of awareness or training in supportive interventions is often the key reason why these therapeutic processes lead to negative outcomes. This book aims to address that gap by offering practical approaches for therapists to navigate these situations more effectively.

While there are many books on supportive therapy, such as those by Markowitz (2022), Novalis et al. (1993), and Winston et al. (2012), among others, this book offers an open-ended supportive therapy approach that stands out as the only approach that is psychodynamically informed. It utilizes a comprehensive psychoanalytic formulation to understand the patient's relational patterns and internal world, but instead of focusing on exploration, it uses this understanding to guide supportive interventions. Unlike other methods, it is open-ended rather than time-limited, and it employs free association rather than being strictly goal-oriented. This unique combination allows for a more flexible and deeply attuned therapeutic process, tailored to the patient's immediate needs while remaining grounded in psychodynamic principles.

This book provides a thorough exploration of key psychoanalytic concepts, empowering therapists from other modalities to apply supportive therapy confidently while deepening the understanding of psychodynamic practitioners. Topics such as object relations, the unconscious, transference, countertransference, the Oedipus complex, resistance, defence mechanisms, symptom formation, the facilitating environment, and the depressive and paranoid-schizoid positions are all covered. These concepts are explained in a way that bridges theoretical depth with practical applicability, with the intent of making the book accessible and useful for a diverse range of clinicians.

Central to the book is a detailed examination of the therapeutic alliance in supportive therapy. It discusses how a strong therapeutic relationship, characterized by trust, empathy, and flexibility, is crucial for patient engagement and retention, but also—and perhaps the key factor—a specific way of listening to the patient's afflictions through a psychodynamic understanding. The book also addresses common challenges in maintaining this alliance, particularly in the early stages of therapy, and provides practical strategies for overcoming these obstacles. Through case studies and clinical examples, the book illustrates how supportive therapy fosters a supportive environment that helps patients navigate complex emotional landscapes, ultimately leading to a more fulfilling and sustainable therapeutic experience.

Overview of Supportive Therapy

Supportive therapy has long been a cornerstone of psychotherapeutic practice, prioritizing the therapeutic alliance and a flexible approach tailored to the patient's needs. Unlike brief, time-limited therapies, supportive therapy fosters a sense of security and reliability through its open-ended framework, significantly enhancing patient engagement and reducing the risk of early termination. This adaptability ensures steady support during crises, whether stemming from external circumstances or the patient's own complex attitudes toward the therapeutic process.

Contemporary therapeutic frameworks are increasingly shaped by systemic pressures rather than clinical evidence or therapist preferences. During my time managing a CBT clinic in London, I observed a persistent misconception, assuming that even CBT, which is the most guided intervention, could be rigidly applied within a standardized timeframe. In reality, therapists consistently emphasized the need for flexibility to address individual needs, a principle often undermined by institutional demands. A similar challenge arises in psychodynamic therapy within NHS adult services, where patients frequently begin making meaningful progress only to face premature termination due to systemic constraints. These time restrictions create barriers to patient security and hinder the therapeutic process.

It is important to clarify that open-ended therapy does not equate to indefinite or unnecessarily prolonged treatment. Rather, it allows therapy to continue until the patient reaches a more stable and resilient state. At that point, termination or referral to a more exploratory approach may be the most appropriate step. This process is not defined by a fixed number of sessions but instead by therapeutic insight. The key advantage of an open-ended framework is that it removes the pressure of an impending endpoint, allowing both therapist and patient to focus on the therapeutic work without the stress of a looming separation.

This issue has become increasingly prevalent in the UK, as we not only face continues cuts on the number of sessions we can provide, but also as psychotherapeutic services have evolved to address individuals with greater levels of disturbance. The NHS and charitable organizations often blur the distinction between suitable and unsuitable candidates for therapy, placing therapists in situations where traditional psychotherapy may not be the most appropriate intervention. This leaves the therapists to navigate mismatches between patient needs and traditional methods. Supportive therapy emerges as a pragmatic response, bridging the gap between patient vulnerability and therapeutic expectations.

Supportive therapy's strength lies in its versatility. Research demonstrates its effectiveness for a wide range of psychiatric conditions, including mood and anxiety disorders, schizophrenia, personality disorders, and substance use disorders (Van Den Beldt et al., 2021). When supportive interventions are applied under such complex circumstances, rather than focusing on symptom reduction, they create a safe space to strengthen coping mechanisms, improve functioning, and enhance quality of life (Hellerstein et al., 1994; Novalis et al., 1993; Pinsker, 1997). As a paradox, not focusing on the symptoms might help reduce the symptoms.

For instance, Hass and Ardell's (2020) research on academic settings shows that students perform significantly better when they feel supported. Their attitudes towards life and their professional and social responsibilities also shift positively. This principle extends beyond academia to all areas of life, underscoring the transformative power of consistent emotional support. Support becomes a key element in the patient's progress; rather than directly intervening in the problematic areas, therapeutic support empowers the patient, fostering a sense of agency that enables them to make meaningful improvements in other aspects of their life. Research, like Roberts Wallerstein (1989), has shown that supportive therapy works through a complex interplay of transference dynamics and external reinforcement that can achieve significant, lasting modifications in personality, symptoms, and functioning, comparable to expressive or analytic treatments. He also found that psychoanalysis and expressive therapies rely more on supportive elements than acknowledged.

This is particularly valuable for patients who struggle to maintain relationships, experience social isolation, or react with hostility under stress. For these individuals, the therapeutic relationship itself is a crucial stabilizing force. If the experience of support is positive, the patient may later transition to other forms of therapy that allow for deeper self-exploration. However, this can only happen after they have had a foundational experience of therapeutic support during their time of need. Wallerstein (1989) found that, without being fully aware, therapists tended to shift towards a more supportive therapeutic approach and move away from the classical setting when working with more disturbed patients.

The reason for this is that retention remains a critical challenge in mental health care. Studies reveal alarming dropout rates: 24% within six months in training therapies (Hamilton et al., 2009), rising to 67% when the patient has a diagnosis of borderline personality disorder (Horner & Diamond, 1996). These figures reflect a systemic failure to engage patients who lack the ego strength for interpretative work or find directive approaches like CBT emotionally inadequate. What I keep seeing when supervising students is that when the patient becomes challenging, the student uses the framework they have been told to use. They try to interpret the patient's unconscious reason for being challenging, hoping the will feel relief, by understanding better, and when I was managing CBT therapist, they will push with exercise, sometime overlook the clear emotions of the patients, or the way they were relating to them, because of the agenda they had.

I could see how patients who left, were scared away or profoundly misunderstood. Patient leaving will always be part of the work, but in these cases, we can see how the issue was linked to what the therapist was offering. The most common mistake, in brief therapies, was the therapist pushing to have an aim for the process: a topic or an area the patient needs to choose on which they can focus the treatment. When the patient reacts to the rigidity, therapists tend to double down on technique, encouraging patients to explore areas, even when it's apparent they're resistant or not yet willing to engage with those feelings.

Supportive therapy directly addresses this gap. By prioritizing emotional containment and alliance-building over rigid agendas, it mitigates the risk of early termination. The therapist's role shifts from problem-solving to fostering a safe, non-judgemental space where the patient feels heard. Particularly in early stages of therapy, establishing a strong therapeutic connection is essential for patient engagement and retention (Swift & Greenberg, 2012). It provides a clear therapeutic setting while avoiding overcomplicated theoretical constructs.

Feeney and Van Vleet (2010) further highlighted that therapist availability, non-intrusiveness, and encouragement are essential for successful therapy, often outweighing specific strategies or formulations. Winnicott (1955) underscored the importance of adapting psychoanalytic techniques to prioritize the therapeutic setting. I would argue that connecting with the patient is more essential than any specific technique or theoretical framework, including neutrality and abstinence from the therapist. This is why supportive therapy focuses on the various ways in which a strong therapeutic relationship can be effectively established and maintained.

This is not a unique characteristic of supportive therapy, as research by Ablon and Jones (1998) and Castonguay (1996) has shown how prioritizing the therapeutic relationship over adherence to technique is linked with better outcomes. Less rigid psychodynamic and CBT practitioners, who adopted a flexible approach, saw improved results compared to those who adhered strictly to structured techniques. These studies emphasize the importance of a positive therapeutic alliance and the value of allowing the patient to guide their own process. They show how the therapeutic tools cannot replace the important of nuanced human connection. As Steiner (1993) stated, sometimes feeling understood is more important than understanding.

When considering where supportive therapy fits within the therapeutic landscape of psychoanalytic interventions, it is essential to examine the general principles of different treatment approaches and understand their respective strengths and limitations. Various therapies fall under the umbrella of psychoanalysis or psychoanalytically informed interventions, including psychodynamic counselling, psychodynamic supportive intervention, psychodynamic therapy, and psychoanalysis. Supportive therapy specifically falls within the category of supportive intervention, emphasizing flexibility, patient engagement, and long-term emotional support:

Intervention	*Times per week*	*Characteristics*	*Patient suitability*
Psychodynamic counselling	once per week	Offers a safe space to think about the external and internal world. Not appropriate for patients with moderate or severe personality, mood, or psychotic disorders. Usually implemented in school or for work-related conflicts.	Patient seeking to gain insight into a specific issue that is not deep rooted in their personality.
Brief therapy and dynamic interpersonal therapy (DIT)	Once per week, for up to 20 sessions	Focus-based and problem-solving, or narrow to understanding and exploring patients own and others' thoughts and feelings to improve relationships and behaviour. Aim at identifying and work through core relational patterns.	Patient suffering from interpersonal problems and with time restrictions.
Supportive therapy	1–2 times per week	Skilled psychotherapists draw on their understanding of the therapeutic alliance and psychoanalytic principles to create a supportive space for patients navigating crises or emotional turmoil.	Patient experiencing a complex moment who requires emotional support.
Psychoanalytic psychotherapy	2–3 times per week	Uncovers unconscious dynamics by actively engaging with the transference, the patient's relational patterns and emotional responses projected onto the therapist.	Patient seeking a deeper understanding of their relational patterns and unconscious conflicts.
Specialized psychodynamic-oriented therapy, such as MBT, EMDR, gender, trauma and transference-focused therapy	Varies	Focuses on specific personality disorders or diagnoses. With clear aims like increasing the capacity of the patient to mentalize problems	Patient diagnosed with the specific criteria of the therapy, such as PTSD with trauma therapy or EMDR.

(*continued*)

(continued)

Intervention	*Times per week*	*Characteristics*	*Patient suitability*
Psychoanalysis	3–5 times per week	A more intensive therapeutic process focuses on transference and countertransference, interpreting the development of a deep therapeutic relationship while working with regression and intense feelings of dependency.	Patient willing to engage in an intense work for a long period of time to explore and understand themselves.

In the UK, psychodynamic psychotherapy within NHS services and Lacanian psychoanalysis in private practice are typically offered on a weekly basis. However, the classification of these interventions remains hotly debated: some argue that true psychoanalysis demands multiple sessions per week, while others contend that even weekly sessions qualify under the psychoanalytic umbrella.

This chart presents a somewhat reductive view of therapy, as it does not fully capture how these approaches function in practice or encompass the full range of therapeutic models. My aim is not to impose rigid definitions on clinical settings but rather to provide readers with a framework for situating supportive therapy. Additionally, the depth of therapeutic work often depends more on the therapist-patient dynamic than on session frequency. What matters in the application of supportive therapy is the assessor's clarity regarding the purpose, strengths, and limitations of each approach, as well as their ability to align these with the patient's specific needs. We will explore this further in the assessment section, but for now, this chart serves to position supportive therapy within the broader therapeutic landscape.

Definition

Supportive therapy offers a unique interplay between the psychoanalytic formulation of a patient's capacity to relate and tolerate the supportive process, and a pragmatic, clear technique that prevents early dropouts. It provides methods to ensure that even complex patients feel supported throughout their therapeutic journey, giving a particular place as guidance to the psychoanalytic formulation of the patient.

At its core, supportive therapy integrates elements of traditional psychoanalysis, such as understanding the patient's internal world and utilizing free association, with supportive techniques designed to foster emotional stability and engagement. However, it does not adhere to the traditional neutrality and abstinence that psychoanalytic interventions require. This approach is particularly effective for patients who lack the ego strength required for deeper interpretive work or who find problem-focused therapies like CBT inadequate for their emotional needs.

To determine whether a patient will benefit from supportive therapy, two factors need to be considered: the patient's capacity to relate to the therapist and their current sources of distress.

Consider, for example, a patient with narcissistic traits who may fear being overwhelmed by the therapist, experiencing the therapist's capacity to think or help as a threat. This can lead to relational patterns marked by envy, dependency, or avoidance (Britton, 2018). Similarly, Rosenfeld (1987) described *thin-skinned* narcissistic patients, a concept echoed by Britton (2018) and Lemma (2009), who highlighted their hypersensitivity to criticism and fear of emotional closeness. Or, such individuals who struggle with intimacy, oscillating between feelings of claustrophobia in close relationships and abandonment in distant ones, a dynamic Glasser (1986) termed the *Core Complex*.

As we know, these patients are not easy to work with and require a high level of experience to establish a therapeutic relationship built on cooperation. Now, consider what happens if the patient has a significant emotional life event: perhaps a separation, a profound rejection, or a serious health concern. The therapist has two conflicts at hand, a patient who is in desperate need of emotional support, at the same time that the patient presents a way of relating that will make the possibility of receiving emotional support too challenging. If the therapist thinks that they can work with the patient's issue with relating, at the same time they offer emotional support, it is a tough approach to offer the patient, who will need amazing resilience to tolerate and benefit from it.

Why? Because working through issues related to closeness, dependency, envy, and jealousy will inevitably create conflict within the couple. In psychoanalysis, this is seen as valuable since, through conflict and its survival, significant growth, maturity, and insight can emerge.

However, the key problem is that the timing may not be right for this patient. A therapist attempting to help in this way may unintentionally push the patient away, as they are not yet ready to engage with such deep conflicts. Instead, the focus should be on providing a supportive therapeutic relationship that meets the patient where they are.

The same happens when patients suffering from a mental health condition require this level of support, and they don't have the resilience for enduring psychoanalytic treatment. (This point will be explored further during the assessment chapter.)

In supportive therapy, flexibility is key to addressing the needs of such complex patients. By creating an adaptable therapeutic environment, it minimizes the risk of premature termination while utilizing psychoanalytic understanding to navigate the intricacies of the therapeutic relationship. The therapist balances emotional availability and validation with the need to avoid colluding with pathological narratives, such as victimization. Studies by McCrady et al. (2002) and Lambert and Barley (2001) underscore the importance of maintaining flexible yet firm therapeutic boundaries to preserve the integrity of the process.

"Flexible" doesn't mean irregular, collusive, or patient-led, as this may not be perceived as a strong therapeutic process by the patient. "Flexibility" means that the therapist can share elements of their life to ease the patient's distress—like talking about things they have in common, offering reassurance, providing advice, and adopting a different approach. The frame, however, is aimed at maintaining a consistent and reliable time and place for the patient, as well as a consistent, friendly attitude from the therapist. (This will be explored later in the book.)

A defining feature of supportive therapy is its reliance on a psychodynamically informed formulation of the patient's internal world and relational patterns. This understanding guides the therapist in selecting interventions that balance support with therapeutic alliance. Supporting the patient does not mean endorsing their pathology; rather, it involves creating a space where they feel heard, cared for, and understood.

The open-ended nature of supportive therapy allows patients to explore their emotions and experiences without the pressure of a fixed timeline. Unlike goal-oriented therapies focused on symptom resolution, supportive therapy fosters deeper emotional and psychological healing. By avoiding the anxieties associated with separation and abandonment, it provides a sense of safety that enables patients to engage fully in the process, ending only when they are truly ready.

The steps of supportive therapy:

1. Setting and Alliance—Starting by establishing a strong and clear therapeutic contract. Defining a setting that addresses the practical aspects of the therapeutic work. This means a clear time, place, and rules, in a way the therapeutic process feels predictable and reliable.
2. Understanding and Expression—Creating a space where the patient feels understood and can express emotions freely. Ideally, the patient should experience the therapist and the therapeutic space in a unique, personal way, unconstrained by rigid superego demands. The focus is not on the content of what the patient brings, but on the resilience of the relationship to endure through their difficult times.
3. Avoiding Repetition—Using interventions, not to uncover the unconscious, but to prevent actions that might lead to early termination due to the repetition of early relational patterns.
4. A Good Ending—Facilitating a mutually agreed-upon ending that is openly discussed and processed over time. The ending should not be enacted impulsively but should leave the door open for the patient to reconnect if needed.

Example of a Supportive Intervention

The different components of supportive therapy will be explored in detail in the following chapters. The reason for presenting a case now is to orient the reader towards what constitutes a suitable case for supportive therapy and to help frame its role within the broader landscape of therapy.

A woman in her 40s came to see me because she was about to be fired. She worked for a complex company that she described as struggling financially and facing staff issues, including constant disagreements and what she perceived as bullying. She found herself in a situation where she might be made redundant but ended up in conflict with her line manager, making it clear that she would lose her job. She had been off sick since, and the way she contacted me was by arriving at my consulting office without an appointment, in tears and despair. I wasn't there, but a message was passed to me, stating how unwell she was. The staff were not concerned for her safety, but they mentioned feeling worried about how sad and distressed she appeared.

From the assessment, it became clear that the patient was repeating a pattern of conflict with authority figures, constantly getting into trouble. She had been fired at least twice before, and in both cases, she saw herself as the victim of a cruel and dishonest male manager. It was also evident that her current manager was trying to resolve the situation, but she misinterpreted everything and felt offended. For example, her manager called her for a meeting, which she described as friendly and aimed at finding a solution, yet she felt singled out because she was the only one called. She was caught in a dynamic where she felt unrecognized and unappreciated, experiencing this as extremely painful. At the same time, she was not considering the emotional consequences of losing her job. She had no active social life, her best friend worked at the same company, and they spent time together at work. Losing her job frightened her because it would mean being alone, but she was unable to acknowledge this while it was happening; her narrative was all about being abused.

When she arrived, she was unable to listen to what I had to say. She would answer my questions but wouldn't wait for me to finish a sentence. My usual approach is not to speak much, so the fact that the few things I did say were disregarded was notable. The most striking aspect of her presentation was that two things were happening simultaneously: first, she had a rigid view of the world; if I even suggested that her repeated experiences might have something to do with her own actions, she would leave. She only accepted a narrative of victimization, and anything outside of that was perceived as victim-blaming. At the same time, her emotional pain and loneliness were palpable. She desperately needed someone to be there for her during this difficult time.

Classical psychoanalytic therapy would aim to establish a stance of neutrality and abstinence, allowing for the exploration of transference and projections, where authority figures mistreat her or let her down, and she, in turn, becomes the victim. This is not too dissimilar to the CBT focus on identifying automatic thoughts, working on cognitive restructuring, developing alternative beliefs to address her victimization, problem-solving skill the patient can learn, among others. If she had greater emotional strength, psychodynamic therapy could have offered her a beneficial long-term outcomes; CBT could had helped if she was looking for change through exercise or learning, not just to be listen to. Brief therapy, on the other hand, would focus on setting a goal to use the time effectively, perhaps reflecting on how she could find a new job or manage her triggers at work. None of the above would address the intense emotional expression of the patient that wants to be listened to.

Supportive therapy, however, begins by building a therapeutic alliance and creating a space where the patient feels heard, with the primary goal of ensuring that therapy remains a supportive presence during difficult times. In this approach, the therapist is less neutral and abstinent, instead adopting a gentler and more supportive stance, avoiding taking sides while ensuring the patient does not feel alone. For example:

Patient "I can't believe this is happening to me. Why doesn't the operational manager remove my manager instead of letting them keep doing this to me?"

My thought was that she saw the operational manager as a parental figure siding with her "siblings" instead of her, representing a repressed conflict where she felt neglected. It also hinted at the transference, where she might be particularly sensitive to moments when she felt ignored or deprioritized by me. In supportive therapy, addressing this directly might not be helpful; instead, the priority is to make her feel supported.

Therapist "It sounds like you don't feel listened to or taken into account."

Patient "It's not that I feel that way—it's that I am not being supported or listened to. They don't care."

Therapist "Hopefully, we can create something here where you feel that I care and that what you're going through matters to me."

Patient "I hope so. Although I'm not sure we can."

As seen here, we are working within the transference by bringing the narrative into the relationship in the present moment. However, the goal is not insight but rather the consistent establishment of a secure therapeutic relationship, reinforcing the message: "This is what you are afraid of—let's work on ensuring it doesn't happen here."

At the same time, saying something like "I hope" or "hopefully" introduces an element of self-disclosure. In traditional psychoanalytic forms of therapy, therapists avoid disclosing their emotions, as the patient's uncertainty about the therapist's feelings is central to the transference work. A more traditional approach might invite the patient to reflect on whether she feels understood in therapy, fostering her projections onto the therapist, that could be perceived as someone who doesn't care either. She might come to unconsciously perceive the therapist as her manager, the operational manager, or ultimately as neglectful parents, thereby revealing her historic anger and struggles. However, this patient was not able to tolerate such exploration. The stress of losing her job was already generating high levels of anxiety; she would not tolerate a therapeutic process that, in order to achieve insight, requires the patient to tolerate more anxiety.

The supportive intervention progressed with the patient frequently checking whether I was on her side. She clearly feared that I would agree with her manager and see her as "difficult." She seemed to be constructing a special relationship with me, one in which it was "her and me against the world." She did this by constantly complaining about others and then assuming I agreed with her point of view. I never actively agreed with her; it's crucial not to collude with the patient's pathology, such as, in this case, reinforce the split between good and bad. Instead, I refrained from challenging her too directly and aligned myself with her emotions rather than her perspective. For example: "I'm sorry that these problems keep happening. You must be exhausted." This statement avoids making a judgement about who is right or wrong but actively validates her emotional experience. I also shared genuine emotions about her struggle, which was particularly useful when she assumed I would be indifferent, and I wasn't.

At one point, she asked me to write a support letter for her employer, stating the emotional damage her manager had caused her. Instead of interpreting my way out of the situation or writing the letter and colluding, I took a firm but compassionate approach:

Therapist "I'm sorry, I can't do this for you. I want to help, but I can't get involved outside our sessions."

Patient "That means you don't really care, doesn't it? It's all talk with you."

Therapist "I see why you feel that way, and I hope we can continue working together so you can see that is not the case."

The temptation in psychodynamic therapy would be to interpret the repetition, help her see how in therapy she is finding herself in another situation were authority figures are failing her. However, a defining characteristic of supportive therapy is avoiding interpretations of negative transference, as the patient would not tolerate them.

Ultimately, this therapy lasted 14 months, supporting her through the loss of her job and her transition to a new one. At the end of our work, I recommended psychodynamic therapy with a colleague, but I never heard back from her. Despite this, I believe I provided a positive therapeutic experience during a critical period in her life.

This is the key takeaway: a patient who would likely be diagnosed with BPD had a constructive and containing therapeutic experience during one of the hardest times in her life. This support may have prevented many impulsive or self-destructive acts, where in moments of desperation and loneliness she could have acted on, but instead brought into our sessions to tell me about them. I could respond with genuine concern, offering a space where her distress was acknowledged and held.

At the same time, the patient didn't gain much insight into her ways of creating conflict when she was working with me. For example, when she told me she would not pay for sessions because she needed to save money, casting me as the bad person who would abandon her in her time of need because I was "all about the money," I could address this directly. I had an open and honest conversation about what she was doing, expressing my hope that she would not sabotage the work we had built together. By doing so, I reinforced the importance of our therapeutic relationship, but no insight was gained during this window of opportunity to understand the nature of her unconscious conflict.

These challenges are easier to navigate when I am not bound by a strictly neutral and abstinent stance, relying solely on interpretation to resolve them. Instead, a more flexible, engaged approach allowed me to provide the kind of support she needed at that moment.

Why Was Supportive Therapy Suitable and Effective?

Supportive therapy was particularly useful for this patient because what she needed at that moment was not deep exploration (that I am not sure she is suitable for) but a stable therapeutic presence. She was seeking someone to be with her until she could regain stability.

This case highlights two crucial elements when thinking about supportive therapy:

1. The impact of life events on emotional functioning.
2. The individual's capacity to engage in a therapeutic process.

I will finally compare the two approaches so the reader could see when supportive therapy should be recommended.

Classical Psychodynamic Approach

- Focus: Transference analysis and uncovering repressed conflicts (e.g. parental dynamics projected onto the therapist and work through).
- Method: Neutrality, abstinence, and exploration through interpretation, not exclusively, but as a main tool.
- Risk: Premature interpretations could overwhelm the patient, reinforcing her sense of being "misunderstood" rather than providing the support she needed. As we have seen patients presenting with emotional instability tend to drop out of treatment, with less than 40% staying more than 3 months. Leaving them with another negative experience and no one to talk to.

Supportive Therapy

- Focus: Immediate emotional support, stabilization, and alliance-building.
- Method:
  - Validation Without Collusion: Acknowledging her distress without reinforcing distorted narratives (e.g. "not challenging her victim role, at the same time that the focus can be the emotional impact of it, without agreeing with it").
  - Transference Management: Addressing fears of abandonment with reassurance ("I want to ensure our therapy lasts for you") rather than interpretative interventions or allowing regression.
  - Boundary Setting: Declining inappropriate requests (e.g. writing a support letter) while reaffirming therapeutic commitment, making the setting feel strong by its predictability and boundaries.

References

Ablon, J. S., & Jones, E. E. (1998). How Expert Clinicians' Prototypes of an Ideal Treatment Correlate with Outcome in Psychodynamic and Cognitive-Behavioral Therapy. *Psychotherapy Research, 8*, 71–83.

Bion, W. R. (1962). *Learning from Experience*. Heinemann.

Britton, R. (2018). *Sex, Death, and the Superego: Experiences in Psychoanalysis* (1st ed.). Routledge.
Castonguay, L. G., Goldfried, M. R., Wiser, S. L., Raue, P. J., & Hayes, A. M. (1996). Predicting the Effect of Cognitive Therapy for Depression: A Study of Unique and Common Factors. *Journal of Consulting and Clinical Psychology, 64*, 497–504.
Feeney, B., & Van Vleet, M. (2010). Growing Through Attachment: The Interplay of Attachment and Exploration in Adulthood. *Journal of Social and Personal Relationships, 27*, 226–234.
Glasser, M. (1986). Identification and Its Vicissitudes as Observed in the Perversions: A Defense Against the Return of a Dreaded Maternal Object. *International Journal of Psychoanalysis, 67*(1), 9–25.
Hamilton, M., Wininger, L., & Roose, S. P. (2009). Dropout Rate of Training Cases: Who and When. *Journal of the American Psychoanalytic Association, 57*, 695–702.
Hass, M., & Ardell, A. (2020). *Supporting Student Mental Health: Essentials for Teachers*. W. W. Norton & Company.
Hellerstein, D. J., Pinsker, H., Rosenthal, R. N., et al. (1994). Supportive Therapy as the Treatment Model of Choice. *Journal of Psychotherapy Practice and Research, 3*(4), 300–306.
Horner, M. S., & Diamond, D. (1996). Object Relations Development and Psychotherapy Dropout in Borderline Outpatients. *Psychoanalytic Psychology, 13*, 205–223.
Lambert, M. J., & Barley, D. E. (2001). Research Summary on the Therapeutic Relationship and Psychotherapy Outcome. *Psychotherapy: Theory, Research, Practice, Training, 38*(4), 357–361.
Lemma, A. (2009). Being Seen or Being Watched? A Psychoanalytic Perspective on Body Dysmorphia. *International Journal of Psychoanalysis, 90*, 753–771.
Markowitz, J. C. (2022). *Brief Supportive Psychotherapy*. Oxford University Press.
McCrady, B. S., Epstein, E. E., Cook, S., Jensen, N. K., & Ladd, B. O. (2002). What Do Women Want? Alcohol Treatment Choices, Treatment Entry and Retention. *Psychology of Addictive Behaviors, 16*(4), 341–349.
Novalis, P. N., Rojcewicz, S. J., & Peele, R. (1993). *Clinical Manual of Supportive Psychotherapy*. American Psychiatric Press.
Pinsker, H. (1997). *A Primer of Supportive Psychotherapy*. The Analytic Press.
Rosenfeld, H. (1987). *Impasse and Interpretation*. Routledge.
Steiner, J. (1993). *Psychic Retreats: Pathological Organizations in Psychotic, Neurotic and Borderline Patients*. Routledge.
Swift, J. K., & Greenberg, R. P. (2012). Premature Termination in Psychotherapy: A Meta-analysis. *Journal of Consulting and Clinical Psychology, 80*(4), 612–620.

Van Den Beldt, H. M., Ruble, A. E., Welton, R. S., & Crocker, E. M. (2021). Contemporary Supportive Therapy: A Review of History, Theory, and Evidence. *Psychodynamic Psychiatry, 49*, 562–590.

Wallerstein, R. S. (1989). The Psychotherapy Research Project of the Menninger Foundation: An Overview. *Journal of Consulting and Clinical Psychology, 57*(2), 195–205.

Winnicott, D. W. (1955). Metapsychological and Clinical Aspects of Regression Within the Psycho-Analytical Set-Up. *International Journal of Psychoanalysis, 36*, 16–26.

Winston, A., Rosenthal, R., & Pinsker, H. (2012). *Learning Supportive Psychotherapy: An Illustrated Guide*. American Psychiatric Publishing.

CHAPTER 2

Introduction to Key Concepts

Introduction to Key Concepts

As Joseph Sandler (1976) explained, Freud's ideas have long been regarded as the foundation of psychoanalytic theory, with many later developments seen as extensions or refinements that must remain consistent with his original work. This perspective reflects a necessary conservatism within psychoanalysis, helping to preserve and protect its core principles. However, psychoanalytic theory has also been in a constant state of organic development, where new insights create theoretical tensions, stretching existing concepts to accommodate evolving understandings. Rather than a fixed and completed system, Freud's legacy can be seen as the starting point for an ever-expanding body of thought, where concepts continuously shift in meaning depending on their clinical and theoretical context.

Sandler (1976) advises maintaining a level of elasticity in psychoanalytic concepts. Since psychoanalysis consists of formulations at different levels of abstraction and part-theories that do not always integrate seamlessly, flexible, context-dependent concepts help create a unifying framework. I also think that many of these concepts were developed in response to specific contemporary issues within society and psychoanalytic thought. When applied rigidly to different contexts without adaptation, they risk becoming mere juxtapositions that fail to make sense of the current problem.

R. S. Escandon, *Contemporary Developments in Supportive Therapy*, Palgrave Texts in Counselling and Psychotherapy,
https://doi.org/10.1007/978-3-031-96059-8_2

In this introduction, I will outline key concepts from both classic and contemporary theory to create a theoretical foundation for the implementation of supportive therapy.

The Unconscious

Alessandra Lemma (2016) explains that Freud used the term unconscious in three distinct ways: descriptively, to refer to mental processes occurring outside of awareness; systemically, as a separate mental system with its own characteristics; and dynamically, as a source of motivation shaped by repressed desires and conflicts. This clear distinction represents the culmination of years of theoretical development, reflecting Freud's evolving understanding of the unconscious.

Even before Sigmund Freud published *The Interpretation of Dreams* in 1900, early papers such as *Screen Memories* (1899) and *The Psychical Mechanism of Forgetfulness* (1898) presented a deceptively simple yet complex question: Why do we forget certain things? And in cases where we do remember, why do our recollections take forms that do not necessarily do justice to the actual events that occurred, but instead transform them into something else?

Freud then explored this question by attempting to uncover the reasons behind it. A crucial insight was that individuals, recalling a memory or forgetting, are often unaware of the underlying reasons for their recollection or forgetfulness.

For example, Freud (1899) describes a patient remembered cutting a yellow flower as a child. Freud proposed that both the flower and its colour carried an unconscious meaning unknown to the patient. After listening to his patient's thoughts and association, Freud suggested that the yellow colour was associated with a dress worn by someone important to the individual early life and that cutting the flower symbolized a deeper, unconscious representation, linked to sexuality, such as deflowering as in losing one's virginity.

This was one of Freud's methods for uncovering unconscious meaning, which simply refers to meanings an individual holds but is unaware of. This idea created a paradoxical view of the human mind: one that possesses meaningful thoughts, memories, and associations without conscious awareness of them. Also, these ideas or memories will not just be stored in a part of our memory, but will be able to influence our understanding of our history and ourselves. Freud (1896), in Further Remarks on the

Neuro-Psychoses of Defence, suggests that certain ideas, like erotic desires or shameful memories, will have a conscious origin, meaning that initially the person was aware of them, but at some point, there will be a process of defence or repression that will make such memories unreachable. But the repressed ideas will persist in the unconscious creating different symptoms.

Freud expanded on this in *The Interpretation of Dreams*, where he showed how hidden meanings could be uncovered. He proposed a method of deconstructing dreams into different components, identifying nodal points, elements that stand out as significant, and analysing their meaning through understanding the processes of symbolization, displacement, and condensation. Through creating this method, he began developing two key concepts: censorship and dream work.

Freud theorized that dreams serve, in part, to prevent the sleeper from waking. A simple example is dreaming of eating when hungry, allowing the individual to remain asleep rather than waking up to find food. This suggests that dreams have an adaptive function, enabling a balance between physical needs and rest. There is a need or a desire, such as hunger, and the dream work creates a moment where the individual dreams of eating.

However, Freud observed that beneath their seemingly nonsensical elements, dreams often conceal deeper meanings, as in the case of the patient who recalled a yellow flower. If that patient had been fully aware of his sexual desire as a child, he might have remembered a more direct expression of it. Instead, the memory was altered, symbolized by the flower. This is because a part of the individual is in conflict with their desire, making them uncomfortable with acknowledging it directly. This is a depiction of humanity in early Freud, one that is in constant conflict with who they are and who they think or wish they would be.

Here, two processes come into play. First, censorship: the mind suppresses the disturbing content. Second, dream work: the meaning is disguised through mechanisms like symbolization, displacement, and condensation that create a story whose purpose is the fulfilment of a wish, and, at the same time, that doesn't create a conflict for the individual dreaming.

A teaching example I often use to illustrate this involves two sisters. They are best friends and genuinely happy for each other's successes. However, one begins to do considerably better in life, while the other, though supportive, feels disappointment and envy. That night, she dreams that she and her sister are walking in a forest when her sister suddenly falls into a pond of water. She tries to help her, but her hands are too slippery, she runs for a rope, but each time her sister begins to climb out, the rope breaks. This sequence repeats throughout the night.

What is happening here? The less successful sister might unconsciously feel envy or resentment, but these emotions conflict with her self-image as a loving and supportive sibling; therefore, they need to be kept away from her own self-awareness, as the imagery could be too disruptive and wake her up. To resolve this, rather than dreaming of actively harming her sister, the dream disguises her aggression in the form of helping but failing. Through displacement, the act of harming is shifted into an act of attempted rescue. This way, the dream preserves sleep, preventing the distressing realization of her own hostility from waking her up.

A different example, relevant to supportive therapy, involves a refugee who, as a child, was about to board a boat with her family. Tragically, just before departure, her father was taken away and later executed. At the time, she was left not knowing where he was or if she would ever see him again.

When she later recalled the journey that followed, she described a boat trip that felt unusually long, making multiple stops in countries that didn't quite make sense. When the actual itinerary of the boat was researched, it turned out that the trip had been significantly shorter than she remembered, not stopping in any of the places she thought it did.

Why This Distortion? And More Importantly, Does This Mean Her Memory Is Wrong?

The point here is not that the memory is inaccurate in a factual sense. Freud's work on screen memories challenges the idea that childhood memories are purely historical records. Instead, memories are formed retrospectively, shaped by later emotions and experiences. In this case, her memory of the journey was shaped by her profound feelings of separation and loss. The journey felt unbearably long, so much so that, in her reconstruction of events, extra days and unfamiliar countries were unconsciously inserted into the narrative.

This example illustrates how unconscious conflict shapes our understanding of ourselves. In the context of supportive therapy, this is particularly useful. It shows where the patient is hurt—not by correcting the memory or analysing the distortion, but by recognizing the depth of emotion behind it. The role of the therapist in supportive work is not to interpret but to be present, to listen with an awareness of the unconscious conflict. Even in silence, this understanding transforms the therapist's presence, allowing them to truly hear and hold the weight of the patient's pain.

A few years later, in 1905, Freud published a case that many, including Lacan (1951), Kohon (1984), and Hinshelwood (2013), consider a failure: an example of how not to work. This was the case of Dora, a patient who abruptly ended her treatment after Freud failed to attune to what was happening in the room, becoming overly preoccupied with proving his theories.

As problematic as this case was, Freud used it to introduce his concept of symptom formation. He argued that a repressed memory, often of a sexual, embarrassing, or traumatic nature, could resurface in the form of symptoms through symbolic compromise formations. In Dora's case, he interpreted her persistent cough as the manifestation of a repressed sexual encounter.

What matters here, beyond the case, is that the concept of symptom formation expanded the notion of the unconscious. It provided a framework for understanding psychopathology, not simply as a collection of isolated symptoms but as the consequence of unresolved unconscious conflicts. This marked a significant development in Freud's thinking, shaping the way psychological suffering would be conceptualized in psychoanalysis.

Jumping forward in time and skipping some important developmental points, by 1923, in *The Ego and the Id*, Freud had formulated a more complete model of the psyche, which he called the Structural Model. This model provides greater clarity on how symptom formation works. Freud introduced three key psychic structures: the id, ego, and superego.

He describes the ego as:

> The ego represents what may be called reason and common sense, in contrast to the id, which contains the passions. (Freud, 1923, p. 25)

The ego, theoretically speaking, became a concept that encapsulated previous ideas Freud had introduced, such as the ego-instincts, which combine the functions of repression and self-preservation. The ego acts as a mediator, resolving conflicts between the other two agencies. In a psychologically healthy individual, it operates under the reality principle, balancing the id's demands with external constraints.

The id represents the inaccessible, unconscious part of our personality, where instinctual drives and desires reside. It is entirely unconscious and operates according to the pleasure principle, seeking the quickest way to reduce tension without regard for social norms or morality. Alessandra Lemma (2016) explains how each person possesses a fixed amount of psychic energy. In newborns, this energy is entirely contained within the id, which consists of innate biological drives, primarily sexual and aggressive in nature. Drives are internal biological forces that seek release, with their buildup leading to discomfort and their discharge bringing a sense of pleasure.

From this point forward, the baby is in a developmental process to find ways in which they can develop an ego that will basically help them adapt to their environment.

Finally, the superego replaces what Freud (1923) had previously referred to as censorship. The reason for this shift in terminology is that Freud came to see the superego as an internalized, punitive authority, rather than a simple mechanism of repression. The superego enforces moral and societal rules, embodying the harsh, judgemental voice of authority within the individual. Depending on the experience the individual has had with authority growing up, the superego can be punitive, sadistic, or cruel.

Freud then proposed that anxiety arises from the ego's struggle to navigate the conflicting demands of the id, which represents instinctual drives and desires, the superego, which imposes strict moral judgements and internalized authority, and the external world, which sets practical limitations. This conflict creates psychic tension, as the ego attempts to manage these opposing forces, leading to symptoms and psychological distress

A modern take on this concept has not changed much. Unconscious fantasies are still considered structured compromises between drives, defences, and superego demands. They manifest in symptoms, character traits, and transference dynamics (Rangell, 1988).

What modern perspectives have incorporated more effectively is how these dynamics manifest in transference, as presented by Sander Abend (2008). In therapeutic work, unconscious fantasies or conflicts are restructured within the therapeutic relationship. That is to say, the therapeutic relationship becomes a catalyst for these fantasies to repeat or reflect themselves. The therapist assumes that unconscious fantasies and processes are at play, inferred from the patient's material, what they say, how they behave in the session, the feelings they evoke, recurring patterns they develop, and more. Abend distinguishes between two types of unconscious fantasies: historical fantasies, rooted in childhood experiences, and contemporary fantasies, which emerge within the current therapeutic relationship.

This brings us to the role of the unconscious in supportive therapy. A patient's unconscious fantasy plays a crucial role in shaping transference and ultimately influences the success or failure of treatment. In this context, concepts like the superego become particularly useful, offering a theoretical framework that nurtures empathy, especially when a patient is engaged in self-punishment. Self-hatred is a common response in bereavement and other distressing circumstances, and understanding the superego can help us navigate these dynamics more effectively.

In *New Introductory Lectures on Psycho-analysis* (1933), Freud explores the superego as an internalized voice that is harsh, judgemental, and excessively critical. He distinguishes it from the ego, emphasizing that while the superego can be critical of others, its primary target is the ego itself. This distinction allows us to conceptualize a part of the mind dedicated to self-judgement, self-punishment, and the imposition of ideals. By framing the superego as an internalized critic, Freud makes the dynamics of self-observation and internal conflict more comprehensible.

Freud (1933) also describes the superego as particularly aggressive and cruel, especially during episodes of depression:

> During a melancholic attack his super-ego becomes over-severe, abuses the poor ego, humiliates it and ill-treats it, threatens it with the direst punishments, reproaches it for actions in the remotest past which had been taken lightly at the time—as though it had spent the whole interval in collecting accusations and had only been waiting for its present access of strength in order to bring them up and make a condemnatory judgement on their basis. (p. 61)

Here, Freud illustrates the internal dynamic of self-hate, depicting the mind as inhabited by conflicting voices engaged in a cruel dialogue.

This can help the therapist understand why many patients feel they don't deserve to be okay or why they consistently avoid opportunities to create a calmer, more fulfilling life.

It is extremely common to find in patients a pervasive sense of guilt without a clear memory attached to it. I don't necessarily mean that a specific wrongdoing has been forgotten, leaving only shame or guilt, though this can certainly be the case. More often, what I encounter is a deep-seated feeling that a transgression has occurred simply by virtue of the patient being who they are. At other times, it is a false sense of responsibility over incidents that were completely out of their control.

In supportive therapy, it is important to understand the theory of a punitive superego since this helps the therapist see that beneath the patient's anger, judgement, sadism, and other strong affects; regardless of whom they are directed at, these feelings remain a part of the patient's unconscious dynamic way of being. As Freud invites us to consider, at some point these emotions will inevitably be turned both against themselves and towards the therapist.

The biggest takeaway is that Freud (1915) describes the unconscious as a dynamic system, not merely a passive storage of forgotten material but an active structure governed by its own principles. He explains that unconscious ideas persist as memory-traces, shaping thoughts and behaviours without entering awareness. At the same time, affects and feelings function as processes of discharge, manifesting as sensations rather than stored representations.

While ideas remain latent and can be reactivated, emotions are experienced directly, often without a clear connection to their original source. This explains why unconscious conflicts can emerge as intense feelings, even when the individual has no explicit memory of their origins.

This means that when the therapist attempts to provide a supportive space, the patient may experience a range of feelings and reactions, many of them negative, such as anger, fear, or frustration. In classical psychoanalysis, the expression of these unconscious emotions is seen as an opportunity to reconstruct past experiences or create a present representation of them, ultimately helping the patient free themselves from these intense reactions.

The challenge in supportive therapy, however, is that the patient may not be in a state where exploration is feasible. Instead, the therapist must bring a psychoanalytic understanding of the situation with a different goal: protecting the therapeutic relationship and restoring communication when the patient begins to withdraw. Many patients, when faced with potential conflict in therapy, prefer to retreat rather than engage, even more when therapy was meant to be a safe haven during challenging times. Having an awareness of the possible unconscious fantasy at play, and a theoretical framework to help the therapist avoid taking it personally, can be invaluable in maintaining a meaningful connection and providing effective support.

An example of this can be seen when a patient is going through a life-changing event, such as adjusting to a disability after an accident or experiencing a profound loss. They will have many emotions in response to these events, emotions that shift from session to session, often contradicting each other. A patient may, for instance, blame others one moment only to turn that blame on themselves soon after.

During this emotional turmoil, the therapist who approaches their role purely as one of exploration may inadvertently irritate the patient and become the target of these fluctuating emotions, not necessarily uncovering a negative transference but rather provoking it. At the same time, if the therapist fails to reflect on these emotions and their significance for both the patient and them, they risk becoming caught up in an enactment.

The proposition is for the therapist to maintain a thinking space in their own mind, where the body of theories presented here can help them conceptualize what is happening in the room. This does not necessarily mean directing observation towards exploration or interpretation, but rather using it as a guide to navigate what is happening in the room, a way of understanding their countertransference and their reactions. By doing so, the therapist can help preserve a sense of safety and containment, both for themselves and for the patient.

Object Relations

Thomas Ogden (2012) argues that *Mourning and Melancholia* marks the beginning of object relations theory because, in this paper, Freud explored how the unconscious is structured around internal object relations, where split-off parts of the ego form enduring, complex relationships. Ogden highlights that Freud's insights into mourning and melancholia laid the foundation for understanding how internalized relationships with lost or conflicted objects shape the psyche.

When we lose someone, that person is not simply forgotten; in fact, quite the opposite happens, they become central to our inner world through memories, daydreams, emotions, and more. The question then arises: if that person is gone, with whom are we actually relating? Is it a memory, an idea, a representation, or something else entirely? By exploring mourning, loss, and melancholia, Freud (1917) described how, in melancholia, an external loss is replaced by an unconscious internal object relationship, where love and hate become entangled, creating pathological bonds. Freud then describes an omnipotent element to unconscious thinking, which seeks to control or embody the lost object, and ambivalence towards the internal lost object.

After Mourning and Melancholia, Freud (1923) underscored how the ego can precipitate the abandonment of object cathexes which, for Alessandra Lemma (2016), implies a deeply *relational* structure, in contrast to the traditional view of Freud as primarily drive-focused. This is an important move from understanding humans as instinct-driven in conflict with a forbidden society to that of relational beings that are not indivisible from the external gratifying or frustrating world.

Object relations theory presents a complex interplay between internalized figures and external relations to caregivers and others. It is a way of looking at the mind as fundamentally structured by internalization of significant relationships as objects between self and other built progressively from early in life. These internalized relationships are not mere memories but dynamic, enduring mental representations that shape an individual's emotional and relational life in the present. These internalized relationships function as dyadic units, consisting of self-representations and object-representations linked by the affect in which they were originally experienced (Kernberg, 2004).

Think, for example, about the superego. As described above, it is possible to see how the interaction between an individual's desires and societal expectations creates conflict. Prohibitions are internalized, and punishment can occur in the form of emotions like shame. This illustrates how the structure of the mind develops through an ongoing interplay with the external world, where different experiences are internalized and linked to a complex network of affects.

Otto Kernberg (2015) proposes that, from the earliest months of life, individuals differentiate between self and others, with self-object representations forming under the influence of peak affective states. When positive relational experiences dominate, self and object representations integrate into whole, cohesive structures. However, if negative experiences prevail, the mind may rely on primitive defence mechanisms, such as splitting, to prevent overwhelming distress, leading to identity diffusion. This will be explore further under the section Defences.

This aligns with Fairbairn's proposition that healthy parenting fosters an outward orientation in children towards real people who can provide genuine contact and interaction. In contrast, a struggling child may become dependent and turn away from the real world, governed by internal fantasies in a pathological manner, one that doesn't let them relate freely (Mitchell & Black, 1995). This highlights the important interplay between the external and internal worlds as a means of relating, demonstrating how object relations theory can serve as a valuable framework for understanding patients' ways of relating to others and to the therapist.

For example, consider a woman who has developed a punitive superego after feeling ashamed of her sexuality (as in the previously mentioned example). When trying to relate to others intimately, she is likely to struggle with the freedom to do so, as she brings an internal fantasy of shame into those interactions. This may manifest in various ways, such as thoughts like, "Am I pretty enough?" or "Would they find me attractive?" These fantasies revolve around the question of "How am I being looked at?" The answer is often critical, as she may constantly feel judged, reminiscent of her experiences of criticism in childhood. This pattern of relating may also extend to other areas; for instance, she may feel ashamed to open up to a male therapist, thus bringing this conflict into the transference.

This will be in line with Klein's notion of the formation of the superego to early introjections of objects and experiences of aggression, indicating that it develops in tandem with the child's relational experiences. The superego incorporates contradictory aspects, including both excessive goodness and severity (Bronstein, 2001). Goodness in this case might represent a rigid notion of purity.

Attachment Theory and Object Relations

The Tavistock Child Development Research Unit, in the late 1940s, highlighted concerns about the emotional and psychological impact on young children when separated from their primary attachment figures, particularly their mothers, as John Bowlby (1960) noted. He explained that children between the ages of 12 months and 4 years universally react with shock and anxiety when removed from their attachment figures and placed with strangers, unless they have already experienced significant deprivation or are unwell. Bowlby expressed frustration with alternative theories that downplay or contradict the significance of these observations. This led to the development of attachment theory, which provides a framework for understanding the relational dynamics between infants and their caregivers, and the role they play in regard to separation and security.

This led to the understanding of different styles of attachment that individuals develop in relationships. A person can feel a secure attachment when feeling comfortable with intimacy and is able to depend on others while allowing others to depend on them. In contrast, they can feel anxious, desperate for closeness and constantly seeking approval of others, usually fearing they will not be good enough or/and that relationships will not last. Others might adopt a false independence, where people distance themselves emotionally from others, feeling safe only through self-sufficiency. Lastly, they could struggle to form any cohesive way of relating and, as a consequence, struggle to see how they relate to others and how people react and relate to them, experiencing relationships as more unpredictable (Bowlby, 1973).

Otto Kernberg (2015) sees attachment theory as a behavioural parallel to psychoanalytic object relations theory and emphasizes the relationship between early attachment experiences and the formation of internalized object relations. Suggesting, that it can provide a framework for understanding how infants relate to their caregivers in terms of emotional and behavioural responses, shaping the child's psychological development and their capacity for forming future relationships.

So, in attachment theory, the concept of secure and insecure attachments reflects the quality of the child's interactions with their caregivers. Secure attachment is characterized by consistent and emotionally accurate responsive caregiving, which fosters a sense of safety and trust in the child. This secure base allows children to explore their environment and develop autonomy while knowing they can return to their caregiver for comfort and support. In contrast, insecure ambivalent attachments emerge from inconsistent caregiving, and insecure avoidant attachments arise from routinely emotionally unresponsive/rejecting caregiving. These styles are associated with difficulties in emotional regulation and relationships later in life.

A securely attached child internalizes positive representations of themselves and their caregivers, leading to healthier relationships and a stable sense of self. Conversely, a child with an insecure attachment may internalize negative representations, resulting in maladaptive relational patterns and challenges in self-esteem.

All of this invites us to reflect on the consequences when things go wrong for so many patients. I recently published (2023) a book chapter titled *Neurobiological and Psychoanalytic Reflection on the Early Stages of Development*, where I explore the impact of early impingement on the development of emotional and cognitive capacities. The developmental moment in which traumatic events occur is extremely important. Depending on their stage of development, an infant can experience negative events as disruptive to their sense of self. This depends on the ego's capacities (Abram, 1996) (the infant's cognitive and emotional maturity), and such events can have lifelong consequences. This is especially true when the events are intense and the infant is not emotionally able to process them, leading to the use of primitive defences like denial or foreclosure. These defences create a tendency for individuals to cope with future stress using the same strategies, potentially causing problems later in life (Abram, 2022).

This understanding becomes crucial when applying supportive therapy. The therapist needs to attune to the patient's distinctive way of being in the world, which influences the dynamics of their encounter, and avoid relying on a prescriptive therapeutic stance that might have worked with others. Having a clear sense of a patient's way of relating and defending can make the difference between a patient feeling distressed by therapy or feeling supported.

Negative reactions are common when individuals feel threatened. In such cases, the individual often resorts to defences rather than stimulating memory, positive feelings of closeness, or a positive sensation after being listened to, leading to defensive reactions such as denial of reality or disconnection from the experience of being alive. This may result in what Winnicott (Abram, 1996) described as an intellectual defence disconnected from somatic experience. Patients may then be physically present in the room but do not engage emotionally with the process because they find it too threatening. Such dissociations, as noted by authors like Lesley Caldwell and Angela Joyce (2011), may result in a loss of creativity. Without authentic connection, the patient's ability to engage with the therapeutic process and feel supported will be limited.

Basic Fault

Michael Balint (1979) furthers this way of understanding emotional development and how things can go wrong for a child as a consequence of inadequate and harmful experiences with caregivers. This could lead to experiencing what he calls a "basic fault" during early relationship that will manifest in adulthood, in the inability to maintain healthy relationships and the stress of relating. He brings an understanding of the importance of the therapeutic role, especially with regard to regression. He describes this occurring when the patient feels safe, and allows the basic fault to be revealed and modified.

One of my patients grew up with two emotionally unavailable parents, which led him to feel inadequate and to blame himself for his parents' lack of attention. This resulted in a belief that others would inevitably react to him with the same dismissiveness. He often made fun of himself, anticipating that people would not take him seriously. Over time, his sensitivity to feeling unimportant became apparent, and it was then possible to pick up on this and create space for him to discuss it. For instance, if I removed my glasses to clean them or took a sip of water, anything that distracted my full attention from him would provoke feelings of fury and being ignored. I was fortunate that he was able to work through these feelings and was open to discussing them.

The difficulty of certain experiences being more damaging for some individuals, compared to others, can be understood through Winnicott's classification of infants. He discusses two types: one who finds pleasure even among disintegration due to sufficient caregiving, and another who experiences "gross impingement," where protection becomes the only viable response. In the latter case, the infant's focus shifts from exploration and play to excessive self-protection in response to external stimuli, distorting their perception of reality and resembling dissociative episodes during trauma (Abram & Hinshelwood, 2018). Lesley Caldwell and Angela Joyce (2011) highlights the significance of this loss of creativity. This dynamic can create a binary perspective on humanity: one path involves perceiving life as something to defend against, while the other embraces life as something to explore.

If we consider "impingement" a form of trauma, we can draw upon extensive neuroscience research regarding trauma's impact on communication and experience articulation. Theories surrounding language inhibition during stress (Cozolino, 2014) illustrate moments of terror when individuals lose the ability to articulate their experiences during and after trauma. Neurobiological studies have shown the inhibition of Broca's area during and post-trauma, which impedes both articulation and memory retrieval, leaving individuals struggling to express or connect with certain aspects of their existence, including their emotions and their connection to the environment. Complications arise when these experiences occur before Broca's area is fully developed, necessitating alternative strategies for infants.

These strategies can be viewed as defensive reactions in the absence of language, driven by emotional responses. Damasio's (2010) theory of "affective systems" explains how various brain areas and neurotransmitters create a complex neural structure crucial for generating and regulating emotions. Emotional responses provoked by traumatic events can compromise future emotional regulation. Damasio refers to this as the theory of automatic emotional responses, where individuals react instinctively before they can articulate or even comprehend their feelings.

This means that a patient coming to see a therapist might perceive the therapeutic environment as threatening, leading them to react defensively and impulsively, regardless of whether the situation is actually positive or negative. Damasio (2010) distinguishes between feelings, the conscious experience of emotional responses, and emotions, which are more automatic, subcortical processes. Feelings arise from brain structures associated with emotions communicating with the prefrontal cortex, leading to the subjective experience of emotions. This reveals a significant aspect of unconscious functioning; individuals do not plan their defences, they react instinctively, shaping their interactions with their environment.

We can connect this with Otto Kernberg's (2004, 2006) theory of two affective systems: a positive affect system linked to prior gratification experiences and a negative affect system associated with pain, which is antagonistic to the positive one. These systems are crucial for developing unconscious motivations and understanding attachment styles, which influence reactions to the environment. Kernberg (2021) identifies emotional, physical, and sexual abuse, abandonment, and chaotic family environments as common traumas with significant consequences during childhood. Early trauma can impair identity formation, emotional regulation, healthy relationships, and trust in others. These impacts may manifest as dysfunctional relational patterns, low self-esteem, trust issues, and impaired empathic responses (Kernberg, 2004).

It is important to revisit the emotional development in which these difficulties occurred to understand why they remain unconscious and out of reach. Freud (1914) explains that from the infant's perspective, there is no clear distinction between the external world and internal perceptions; instead, the infant perceives their environment as an extension of themselves. Freud posits that infants believe the outside world belongs to them, an indivisible part of their being, gradually discovering that this is not the case. Christopher Bollas (1987) suggests that a progression of feeling whole could begin in utero and is fundamentally primitive, representing a fragile and vulnerable moment where the baby engages with the experience of "being" or feels anxious about survival.

Authors like Rosenfeld (1964) describe this as a primary narcissistic relationship, where individuals may deny the existence of anything outside themselves due to separation issues, leading to a lack of recognition of distinct others. Steiner (1993) explains how individuals resist relinquishing a state of omnipotence and control, blurring the lines between self and other. When infants become defensive, they immerse themselves in a state that does not allow for feeling, experiencing, or developing a sense of self, leading to diminished distinction between the external and internal worlds. Consequently, their sense of identity, including the binary process of "other" and "I," becomes more complex when there is no clear sense of self or "I."

During transitional periods (Winnicott, 1971), where the discovery of internal and external can take place, infants can encounter objects they do not consider part of themselves but can possess. Paradoxically, for Winnicott, these objects do not exist externally, as, for the infant, they are not derived from their inner world but can be possessed (like a toy) while simultaneously representing an internal sensation, such as comfort from being near the mother. This creates a transitional space where the object is both internal and external, neither entirely the mother nor merely a toy.

If successful in this transitional space, the child can play, engage with subjectivity, and explore their identity. If not, they may face significant limitations. For instance, the patient who was overly preoccupied with being rejected had not even questioned what they wanted from life, they focused solely on avoiding rejection and felt quite miserable, living an inauthentic existence, where they were striving to be someone not rejectable. Focusing on themselves was something they had never done before. Their way of dressing and the things they liked revealed questions they had never considered about themselves, they were more worried about looking normal in the eyes of others. They reacted to situations without clear self-awareness of why they felt a particular way. This self-awareness requires a solid understanding of the self, enabling exploration of preferences and triggers, characteristics of themselves they hadn't got in touch with. For example, it is very different to be able to say: "when that person made that joke, I was hurt, because I am sensitive to such topic" rather than simply reacting and feeling attacked.

The idea of early trauma and the potential development of the self resonates with what neuroscience calls "critical periods": phases of rapid development when experiences can profoundly influence neuronal maturation. For example, learning to play a musical instrument as a child typically leads to better adult proficiency, as does language acquisition. There are moments when these early opportunities are more evident. Dr. Carla Shatz's (1990, 1992) work at Stanford University focused on brain plasticity related to the visual cortex, explaining the mechanisms associated with critical periods of visual development. Her research earned her the Kavli Prize in Neurosciences in 2016. In her studies, she discovered that if an infant suffers from congenital cataracts between the ages of 2 and 7 years, their visual neural connections will be improperly formed, resulting in lifelong consequences for the binocular development of the visual system.

This is the parallel I am making with many of the authors I am reviewing; how they indicate that early moments in life are crucial for developing a sense of self, distinction between others and self, and relational patterns. When something goes wrong during these formative periods, it creates a defensive state where the individual must navigate their emotional life using inadequate defences. Authors like Bromberg (1993) described the consequence of trauma: "it effectively obliterates, at least temporarily, the existence of that self to whom the trauma could occur, and it is in that sense like a 'quasi-death (pg154)'." It is a way of understanding the "poorly adapted self-representation" as a state of not-being, of dissociation, or partition between a capacity of recognizing part of our consciousness and the self.

Facilitating Environment

A facilitating environment provides the necessary conditions for psychological growth, emotional development, and integration. It encompasses everything the therapist offers to create a safe space for the patient. This includes a consistent setting, a therapist who is reliable and predictable, and a responsiveness that is attuned to the patient's emotions without being reactive. There must also be a level of adaptability that maintains the focus on the patient as the centre of the work.

The concept of a facilitating environment is rooted in maternal holding, which serves as the foundation for symbolic development (Caldwell & Joyce, 2011). This early dynamic allows the infant to experience a state of security where they are not preoccupied with survival, enabling them to engage with their own experiences. Winnicott (1970) emphasized that psychoanalysis is not merely about interpreting the unconscious but about establishing a professional setting that is trustworthy enough for the therapeutic work to take place. Without trust, a patient will not open, as they need to feel that the therapist will be receptive, caring, and competent enough to manage what they bring to the session.

A clear example of this can be seen in patients struggling with suicidal ideation. Many have not disclosed their thoughts to anyone due to the fear that speaking about them will make them act on them. One patient, for instance, was terrified by intrusive thoughts after reading about a person who had jumped in front of a train. He feared that discussing these thoughts would make them more real or push him towards action. His real concern, however, was whether I could manage his distress without becoming overwhelmed and hopeless as at times they felt. Simply voicing his fears within a safe therapeutic space provided him with a sense of relief. The therapeutic space became a room where this and another topic could be addressed safely.

In supportive therapy, a facilitating environment is less about achieving a cure, or emotional growth and more about providing a space of holding and care. The therapist's presence directly shapes the treatment, mirroring the mother-infant relationship (Caldwell & Joyce, 2014). A reliable, adaptable, and consistent setting allows patients to regress safely and re-experience early traumas that were never fully integrated (Abram, 1996). In supportive therapy, the aim is not to foster regression, but the reality is that patients in distress are likely already regressed, seeking a safe and holding space.

The importance of trust in early relationships shapes how many patients relate to others. For those who have experienced unpredictable early attachments, the therapist must offer a level of reliability beyond what they have encountered in their everyday lives, emphasizing the therapist's role in providing care, consistency, and dependability. Another essential aspect of the analytic setting is the recognition of the interdependence between analyst and patient, akin to the mother-infant relationship (Caldwell & Joyce, 2011). For many patients, this interdependence is deeply anxiety-provoking. Their past experiences have taught them that dependency is a source of pain, abandonment, or abuse, making them wary of trusting another. This highlights a central paradox of the facilitating environment: while it is theoretically a space that fosters emotional growth and security, in practice, many patients experience it with ambivalence, reacting almost phobically to the intimacy and emotional vulnerability it entails.

The reason for this paradox is that, as Abram (1996) notes, regression allows the patient to revisit past trauma, process it, and ultimately move forward, but in principle, it brings it back. The reason such traumas feel newly experienced is that they originally occurred at a time when the patient lacked the capacity for integration and relied entirely on an auxiliary ego. As Winnicott (1974) explained in Fear of Breakdown, patients fear past experiences that have not yet been fully processed. He wrote, "The ego is too immature to gather all the phenomena into the area of personal omnipotence" (Winnicott, 1974, p.104).

In a way, this returns to the idea of an unconscious expression of early experience: avenues of relating that shape the patient's emotional life without their awareness. This understanding prepares the therapist to anticipate that, depending on how the patient relates, there will likely be a repetition of these early dynamics in the therapeutic process. For example, a patient with a history of repeated abandonment may initially seek a secure and safe space in therapy yet find themselves experiencing the process as unstable or potentially abandoning under different circumstances, such as during therapist breaks.

In the next chapter on assessment, this will become particularly important. Gathering a thorough history of the patient's relationships with their nuclear family, friends, and partners will provide insight into the potential relational turmoil the therapist may encounter. It will also help determine whether the patient might struggle to maintain consistency in a more exploratory therapeutic process and instead require a more supportive intervention.

Oedipus Complex

Freud's conception of the Oedipus complex emerged from his self-analysis and correspondence with Wilhelm Fliess, where he identified unconscious desires for his mother and rivalry with his father, framed through Sophocles' Oedipus Rex. Freud viewed this complex as a universal "fate," where repressed incestuous desires and patricidal impulses shape neurosis and societal norms. In Totem and Taboo (1913), he mythologized this dynamic, proposing a primal horde where patricide led to guilt and the establishment of societal taboos, internalized as the superego. Freud's theory intertwined ontogenetic (individual development) and phylogenetic (collective inheritance) elements, suggesting repressed memories of ancestral trauma influence behaviour (Freud, 1914, 1918). Across cultures, individuals develop conflicted feelings about their love for their mother and the challenge of sharing this affection with others. This can manifest in fantasies of exclusive possession and the destruction of rivals. The try to possess her and annihilate all competition. Symbolically speaking, it means that society will develop rules and laws that will punish individuals who transgress their rules over who they can have sex with, and who they can kill.

The British School, particularly Melanie Klein, diverged from Freud's phylogenetic focus, emphasizing early childhood and object relations. Klein positioned the Oedipus complex in infancy, linking it to pregenital stages and the infant's relationship with the mother's breast. She described unconscious phantasies of aggression and reparation, arguing the superego forms earlier than Freud proposed, rooted in oral and anal stages (Klein, 1928, 1946). As we will see later in this chapter, the capacity of an individual to manoeuvre into a depressive position will become a key aspect that will determine how they tolerate loss and rejection. By the time the infant encounters the Oedipal triangle, comprising the baby, the mother, and the father, they will have already developed a degree of emotional capacity that helps them tolerate separation and manage their feelings towards an external reality that does not always align with their desires. This process influences their ability to relate to others as whole objects or as part-objects, meaning they may either engage with others as complete individuals or fixate on only certain aspects of the relationship, denying the more threatening elements.

Ronald Britton (1989) expanded the concept of the Oedipus complex by focusing on the child's perception of the parental couple and the unique relationships they form with each parent. He introduced the idea of the "primal family triangle," emphasizing the child's realization of a link between the parents that excludes them, often first encountered in the primal scene (awareness of parental intercourse). This realization can be shocking because it highlights the child's exclusion, their inability to participate, and the fact that they are not the centre of their parents' world.

Britton (1989), following Klein, suggested that early part-object experiences shape how a child tolerates this discovery. If a child already struggles with separation or abandonment, realizing that their mother has independent relationships can trigger deep anxieties. The nature of the parental link, whether loving, hostile, caring, or abusive, becomes a prototype for future relationships.

If the child successfully integrates this awareness, it reshapes their relationships with both parents, allowing them to see them as individuals with separate roles and perspectives. This cognitive shift lays the foundation for genuine empathy, as the child recognizes that others have independent thoughts and emotions.

Britton (1989) also explored how some individuals find the concept of "thirdness" intolerable. He described patients who could not accept differing viewpoints, experiencing them as threats rather than alternative perspectives. In therapy, these patients react defensively, even aggressively, when the analyst expresses an independent thought, revealing the deep-rooted fear of being excluded from an emotional link.

This last point is crucial in managing patients in supportive therapy, as they may only tolerate a therapeutic relationship that operates entirely on their own terms. This can become problematic, as the therapist's independent thinking may be perceived as a threat. In such cases, the theoretical framework of thirdness can help the therapist navigate these complex situations, providing a way to manage the patient's resistance to perspectives that challenge their sense of control.

It is also important to note that Freud's model is a phallocentric one, in which the resolution of the Oedipal conflict is assumed to lead individuals to fall in love with someone of the opposite sex, identify with their own gender, for women to accept their castration, and for men to submit to the law of the father or face castration anxiety. Freud's theory of female sexuality, in particular, has faced significant criticism; with time, the heteronormative approach has also brought a level of scrutiny, with some people accusing Freud of misogyny and homophobia and other defending him, as an author who was simply describing the society of Vienna in the late 1800 and early 1900s. Karen Horney (1933) challenged the concept of penis envy, emphasizing female agency going beyond a simple comparative analysis between the anatomic differences, while Simone de Beauvoir (1997) critiqued Freud's portrayal of women as the "Other," as an individual which will always be defined in society, by relating her role to a man, and what he does or doesn't do. French theorists such as Lacan reinterpreted the phallus as a symbolic function rather than a biological reality (Bailly, 2009), giving a figurative dimension that transcend the anatomy, into a realm of symbolism. Melanie Klein, in contrast, reframed the female Oedipus complex by emphasizing the breast as central to early psychosexual development and understanding penis envy as a displacement of maternal disappointment (Klein, 1945). In a way, she argued that Freud was not necessarily wrong in being phallocentric, but his theory was incomplete as is the early relationship with the breast what will give a meaning to the phallos, in a way change the view from phallocentric to breast-centric.

Freud's Oedipus complex not only generates controversy, but was politicized as a tool to enforce heteronormative patriarchy. Post-Freudian thinkers, such as Deleuze and Guattari (1972), rejected the Oedipus complex as a capitalist tool repressing desire, where people are pushed to obey social norms through the incorporation of requirements to become consumers and producers. Authors like Slavoj Žižek (2018) linked modern neurosis to societal pressures for happiness as the new social norm, using the concept of the Oedipus complex as a way of understanding how societies impose their will on the individual, with the individual then internalizing it as their own.

The Depressive and Paranoid-Schizoid Positions

Klein (1946) posited the paranoid-schizoid position as an early developmental stage in which the infant experiences the world in a highly polarized manner, dividing objects into "good" and "bad" based on feelings of gratification or frustration. For example, if a baby feels distress and is then fed, they may experience themselves and their surroundings as positive due to the gratification received. However, if they suffer from reflux and remain distressed, unable to find relief, they will internalize a negative experience, not only of their own body but also of others and the early interactions with their caregiver.

This early experience is often represented symbolically through the image of the breast: the breast may be perceived as either withholding and causing suffering or as successfully providing nourishment and comfort. Such early representations are fundamental in shaping the infant's perception of the world. Rooted in instinctual dualism (Roth, 2001), the paranoid-schizoid position reflects the struggle between life and death instincts, with the infant projecting their own feelings of love or hatred onto objects.

Splitting serves as a primary defence against overwhelming anxiety, allowing the infant to project bad aspects outward to expel danger while internalizing good aspects for security. For instance, if the infant experiences the breast as overwhelmingly bad or feels excessive hatred towards it, they may struggle to feed calmly in its presence. However, if they are in the presence of a different breast, one that is not associated with frustration, the experience may be positive, allowing them to feed and sleep without distress. This process requires the infant to develop the capacity to split the negative aspects of feeding away from the experience itself in order to allow themselves to be nourished.

However, excessive reliance on splitting can lead to a fragmented ego, intensely persecutory anxieties, and may necessitate idealization as a compensatory defence. Klein (1946) also emphasizes how these early defensive mechanisms shape later emotional and cognitive development, sometimes manifesting as disruptions in continuity, such as between wakefulness and sleep.

According to Melanie Klein (1935), the depressive position represents a key developmental stage in which the infant moves beyond the extreme splitting of the paranoid-schizoid position and begins to recognize objects as whole and separate. This shift allows for a more integrated view of reality but also introduces feelings of guilt, concern, and responsibility for the loved object.

In the depressive position, the infant realizes that the "good" and "bad" aspects of the mother belong to the same person. This recognition creates anxiety about harming the loved object, as the child acknowledges their own aggressive impulses. Klein (1935) describes how individuals under stress may regress from the depressive position back to the paranoid-schizoid state, avoiding guilt by resorting to splitting and projection. This regression can manifest in paranoid anxieties, where fragmented internalized objects become persecutory.

If the baby is able to come to terms with their experiences during the paranoid-schizoid position, a different kind of anxiety emerges. The term depressive anxiety refers to the anguish of feeling they have damaged the person they love, leading to a preoccupation with reparation. This new perspective on life opens up a more accurate and less partial view of reality. As splitting diminishes, negative experiences become less catastrophic or threatening, and positive ones become less idealized (Gomez, 1997). It encourages the individual to think about the other and consider what the other needs for their relationship to be repaired. This stands in contrast to fearing the other and focusing solely on protection of the self.

Take, for example, a breakup. We have all encountered patients or friends who, after separating from someone, feel the need to paint their ex-partner as a villain. This serves to avoid the anxiety of losing something important in their lives. The use of devaluation and splitting, viewing the ex-partner as entirely bad without recognizing any positive qualities, leaves them with a polarized narrative, full of victims and villains, with no middle ground. This often increases their paranoia because acknowledging any good aspects of the relationship would bring them into contact with a sense of loss they cannot tolerate.

A patient of mine, for instance, had just gone through a divorce and was using manic defences to cope. She was trying to convince both me and herself that she had lost nothing of value. She threw herself into an endless pursuit of exciting nights out, curated a social media presence to prove she was having fun, and insisted she was not missing out on anything. In reality, she was not truly engaging with any of these experiences. Instead, she was consumed by paranoia, constantly imagining a social media audience judging her, not just as "cool" or "not cool," but also as "happy" or "sad." She was desperate to conceal her sadness.

On the other hand, we have also seen people who can sit with their grief, experiencing peaceful tears over their loss. These individuals may not immediately know what the loss means for them, but they are not seeking an easy fix. Instead, they stay with the pain and gradually come to understand its significance. At the same time, they can be worried about the potential damage that each had done to the other. By the end, they could have a memory of the good experience, keeping something positive alive, as Rick Blaine (played by Humphrey Bogart) said to Ilsa Lund (played by Ingrid Bergman) during a pivotal scene in Casablanca (1942):

> We'll always have Paris. We didn't have it, we lost it, until you came to Casablanca. We got it back last night.

Emphasizing that their memories of love are unaffected by the circumstances that forced them apart and will keep them apart. The good elements can stay as such, even if they are no longer a part of one's life.

Britton (1989) suggests that moving through the depressive position allows for the development of symbolic thought, triangulation, and the ability to think empathically. When this process is disrupted, individuals may remain stuck in paranoid-schizoid splitting, struggling with persecutory anxiety and an inability to hold multiple perspectives. This is equivalent to Rick being trapped in a negative narrative of the things that Ilsa did wrong, as a reflection of the inability to confront his loss.

But also, Ronald Britton (1989) takes this idea even further when he explores the depressive position in relation to the development of the triangular space. He understands that this development is crucial to the capacity to tolerate the awareness of separateness between self and others. Britton argues that the depressive position is not solely about guilt and reparation (as Klein emphasized) but also about the ability to recognize and think about the third position. In this phase, the infant comes to realize that the mother has a separate relationship with the father that in the mind of the mother, there is an independent idea of the father, a way of looking at him, that will be different to how they see their own father, therefore and independent mind. For example, if Rick can view Ilsa as a human in conflict, torn between two men, and understand the struggles this represents for her, he is engaging with her in a way that reflects the third position. He is considering her desires and recognizing that her perspective may differ from his, perhaps life with the other wealthy man is more important for her, for instance. In this way, Rick can reflect on her mind and consider what she wants as an independent person. On the other hand, if Rick reduces Ilsa to a negative stereotype, failing to understand their circumstances and instead creating a one-dimensional, defamatory narrative, he is not engaging in the same reflective process. This approach ultimately harms the relationship, as it disregards the complexity of the other person's experience and turns her just into a gold-digger or some other denigrating narrative, in hope of getting rid of his need for her, by devaluating her.

It's also important to consider that the paranoid-schizoid position, though initially a normal stage of early development that matures into the depressive position, is also a recurring experience throughout life. Difficulties in transitioning between these positions can create vulnerabilities to the influence of pathological organizations (Steiner, 1987). The paranoid position is not one that is simply overcome, as if it were just another developmental step a person goes through. Ogden (1992) asserts that the Kleinian paranoid-schizoid and depressive positions should not be viewed from a strictly sequential, linear developmental perspective, but rather as modes of psychological experience that are present throughout life. The paranoid-schizoid position is a state that everyone may utilize when under stress, although pathological structures tend to rely on it more heavily. In contrast, the depressive position is not always accessible to everyone and can be more difficult to reach or maintain.

Finally, as we will see in the following section on defences, Paranoid positions may sometimes be necessary. I recall a case in which a person was about to be laid off. They had a mortgage and various financial obligations, and they openly admitted, *"I am going full manic, applying for every job I can."* The problem was that, in their manic state, they were not submitting good applications or performing well in interviews, so their efforts were not very effective. However, this manic defence still served a purpose, it allowed them to push through the crisis until they eventually found a new job. This highlights an important point: while the depressive position helps people integrate and process loss, manic defences can serve a pragmatic function when sadness is perceived as an unaffordable luxury in that moment. This invites the therapist to reflect on the reason why a patient needs such defences, rather than look for a depressive, reflective stand.

I find this particularly useful when applying supportive therapy. Having an awareness of a patient's emotional position makes a significant difference in how receptive they will be to an intervention. If a patient is already feeling defensive and under attack, any interpretation that highlights a negative aspect of themselves will likely be experienced as criticism and a threat, triggering further anxiety and defences. On the other hand, a patient in a depressive position is more able to take in what is being said without immediately becoming defensive.

Resistance and Defence Mechanisms

Defences are unconscious mechanisms that protect individuals from perceived psychological danger by distorting or avoiding internal and external reality. This can involve threats from within, such as a sexual or aggressive impulse that conflicts with the individual's ideals, or external threats, like receiving news of a loved one's death and falling into denial. Defences help manage internal conflicts between the id, ego, and superego, maintaining psychic equilibrium. However, excessive or rigid reliance on defences can hinder self-awareness and distort relationships with both internal and external reality (Lemma, 2003).

At the same time, defences are essential for tolerating different aspects of life. Freud (1915, 1923, 1927a) extensively explored how individuals struggle to acknowledge the reality of death, which is a fundamental vulnerability of the human condition. Meaning that any ordinary human would need to use some mechanism to manage their anxiety and feelings of guilt around their human condition. Freud (1927b) also suggested that religious beliefs function as a collective defence mechanism, offering an illusion of protection and an afterlife to manage the fear of death:

> There is the painful riddle of death, against which no medicine has yet been found, nor probably will be. With these forces nature rises up against us, majestic, cruel, and inexorable; she brings to our mind once more our weakness and helplessness, which we thought to escape through the work of civilization. (p. 16)

As mentioned, all individuals use defences to cope with the realities of being human. For example, repression plays a crucial role in shaping human relationships. By repressing sexual desires, individuals can develop friendships and family structures without being constantly confronted by feelings of arousal. Another example is a person who dedicates their life to hard work, unconsciously believing that their achievements will allow them to transcend mortality. This defensive rationalization alleviates anxiety about death and will turn such anxiety into something meaningful for them.

However, as Alessandra Lemma (2003) highlights, defences can become too rigid, affecting a person's ability to adapt to reality. For example, the individual mentioned above could become a workaholic. If the defences are too immature or primitive, the individual might struggle to manage their anxiety effectively. For instance, if the repression of a sexual component is unsuccessful, the individual may turn to compulsive behaviours to alleviate their desires, as seen in many cases of obsessive nature.

Poul Rohleder and Deborah Abrahams (2020) classify defences based on an individual's level of psychological functioning. They distinguish primitive defences (such as denial, splitting, projection, projective identification, dissociation, omnipotence, idealization, and manic defences) from neurotic defences (such as repression, regression, undoing, displacement, reversal, isolation, conversion, acting out, rationalization, intellectualization, reaction formation, sublimation, and humour).

All these mechanisms operate in response to extreme anxiety. While psychotic patients rely on primitive defences as a primary mode of functioning, neurotic individuals may resort to them in times of crisis. For example, a neurotic patient experiencing a traumatic event might dissociate, or if faced with a loss, they may temporarily deny it. The key distinction is that psychotic patients rely on primitive defences more consistently.

In psychotherapy, defences are often examined through the concept of resistance, where certain thoughts or emotions are avoided because the individual struggles to tolerate them. Traditional psychoanalytic therapy aims to reduce resistance, helping patients gain insight into unconscious conflicts. However, in supportive therapy, the focus is different. The goal is not to challenge or dismantle defences but to provide a space where the patient feels heard and emotionally contained. A patient can remain in supportive therapy for an extended period while continuing to use primitive defences, without these being confronted by the therapist. The emphasis is on creating a safe environment where the patient can express their needs and be listened to, rather than encouraging exploration or interpretation.

An example of resistance in supportive therapy can be seen in the following case:

> A patient of mine, an 18-year-old, came to see me as his parents believed he needed therapy, after experiencing a small emotional breakdown. His mother had cancer a few years ago, and she had a relapse just a few weeks before his emotional breakdown.

The patient didn't want to speak about his mother's cancer at all; he barely mentioned it during the assessment, and the sessions became focused on girls and friends. It was clear that his fear of losing his mother was present and causing problems, but it is not the role of supportive therapy to address it directly. This doesn't mean that there was no psychodynamic thinking around it that could benefit other interventions, for example, I understood why his friend was such a safe haven in relation to what was happening at home. I also understood why he was fearful of getting close to girls, when they could also become ill. This allowed me to have an emotional connection with the patient, where I could follow the mood and verbal content of the session. To risk sounding repetitive, if the patient could have tolerated talking about his mother's cancer, he would have benefited more from psychodynamic therapy. Discussing it made him feel worse, but this doesn't mean we were ignoring it, we focused on what was keeping him together.

After months, he finally mentioned that his mother's next surgery would be in two weeks, that was all he said. I took this in, asked some questions, and he answered, but not much else happened, as he still didn't want to talk about it. Once the surgery was completed and, a few months later, his mother received the all-clear and he stopped attending sessions.

It was extremely important to provide this space during such a difficult time. This space understood the fragility of his defences and recognized that challenging those defences could lead to extreme anxiety and breakdown. Supportive therapy was about understanding this and not challenging him.

Transference and Countertransference

Broadly speaking, transference refers to the expectations a patient has of their therapist based on past experiences, and countertransference refers to the responses of the therapist to the patient based on those experiences including their emotional content. Both transference and countertransference play crucial roles in the therapeutic process, as they provide insights into the dynamics between therapist and patient.

Freud (1912) explored the dynamics of transference, suggesting that it is not created by the therapeutic situation but rather revealed through it. In transference, past relationships and experiences are repeated within the therapeutic relationship, often due to unresolved unconscious conflicts and repressed feelings or desires. This aligns with Freud's broader concept of the repetition compulsion, wherein unresolved early experiences are not remembered verbally but acted out within the therapeutic relationship (Lemma, 2003).

Freud (1912) shifted his view on transference, moving from considering it an issue to recognizing it as a tool for understanding the repressed unconscious of the patient. He advised that transference should neither be avoided, nor sought out, but interpreted. In this way, the therapist offers the patient a fragment of the experience being projected from past relationships. For example, if a patient, having been hurt by people they trusted in the past, feels fearful of being hurt again when getting close to the therapist, the therapist can help explore the roots of this anxiety, providing a space for reflection.

Transference can thus be understood as the unconscious projection of past relational patterns, particularly from early object relationships, onto the therapist. Anna Freud (1987) viewed transference as a window into past emotional experiences, with defences shaping how patients engage in therapy. This idea is illustrated in David Malan's (1979) case study, where a female patient develops intense, guilt-ridden sexual feelings for her male therapist. These feelings mirror her early relationship with her possessive and emotionally enmeshed father. Unable to integrate love and sexuality, she had spent her adult life either distancing herself from "respectable" men or engaging in secret, guilt-laden sexual relationships with "disreputable" men. Her feelings for the therapist, therefore, were not about him personally but rather a repetition of unresolved longing and guilt related to her father.

Peter Fonagy (2014) expands on Malan's views, emphasizing his commitment to making psychoanalytic concepts systematic, transparent, and empirically grounded. In Malan's approach, transference can be seen as a structured framework that links symptoms to the interplay of defence, anxiety, and impulse. As seen in the case example, above, he considered past experiences, present difficulties, and the therapeutic relationship, together thereby creating a model of transference which emphasizes its dynamic nature. Transference is thus viewed as a tool for insight, helping patients understand their unconscious emotions and desires.

Countertransference has also evolved from an unwanted emotional reaction by the therapist to an important tool for understanding the patient and guiding interventions. Early psychoanalysis saw countertransference as something that should not affect the therapeutic process, if the therapist felt distress or sadness, it was seen as stemming from their own issues rather than from the patient. However, over time, it became understood that the therapist's emotions are crucial, as empathy, ultimately an emotion response form the therapist, is essential to analysis (Sanchez Escandon, 2023).

However, it is also critical to recognize that the patient must be protected from potential projections of the therapist. The therapist, in their attempt to understand the patient, can project their own conflicts onto the patient, as Little (1951) poetically expressed: "We all have our private graveyards, and not every grave has a headstone" (p. 37). As therapists, we use ourselves to understand our patients. Not everything the patient brings can be seen as a projection. As Pearl King (1978) wrote: "I do not, however, assume that every communication between patient and analyst relates directly to transference, and it becomes important to differentiate those feelings and moods which are related to the operation of the transference, from those related to my reactions as a human being working with another human being who suffers from mental pain and who has come to me for help" (p. 331).

An important consideration in modern globalized therapy is the incorporation of culture into the understanding of transference and countertransference. Cultural factors significantly shape both the patient's and clinician's perceptions, emotions, and interactions within the therapeutic encounter. Authors like Fakery Davids (2011) argue that internal racism exists within the psyche of each individual, which becomes particularly relevant in the context of transference and countertransference. In these dynamics, the therapist may unconsciously draw upon their own cultural experiences to understand or reflect upon their patient.

Without awareness of our internal racism or prejudice, therapists risk pathologizing expressions that are culturally normative for the patient. This can lead to misunderstandings, misdiagnoses, and inadequate interventions. To avoid these pitfalls, there must be space for both the therapist's and the patient's cultural identities to interact, understood not through the lens of either culture alone, but as a third perspective that emerges from their dynamic interaction. This perspective treats transference and countertransference as dynamic and co-constructed, influenced by broader social, historical, and cultural contexts (Aggarwal, 2011).

The interplay between individual psychological processes and social and cultural contexts further complicates the dynamics of transference. In transference, individuals often project their past experiences onto others in social groups, reflecting the broader interplay between individual and group dynamics. Freud (1921) discussed this in his concept of group mentality, where personal identities can be overshadowed by collective influences. Dalal (2015) argued that the "I" is shaped by the various "we" groups individuals belong to, suggesting that people absorb the norms and beliefs of overlapping cultures, which in turn shape their development and social interactions. Understanding transference through this psychosocial lens offers deeper insights into the role of prejudice and identity in shaping behaviour within social contexts.

When I am teaching countertransference, and how useful it can be, I tend to give the following example that comes from my experience working with homelessness and substance misuse. I remember a case of a person who suffered from substance misuse, while intoxicated, became quite charismatic—making jokes, pushing boundaries, and constantly getting into small troubles, such as being kicked out of pubs.

I recall seeing patients, shouting in the streets, creating public scenes, and making a big commotion. On multiple occasions, they would say things like, "What are you going to do? Call the cops?"—even when no one had mentioned such a thing. They repeatedly referenced the authorities, as if expecting confrontation.

With time, however, I noticed something interesting. On the surface, they were loud, disruptive, and reckless, but my own emotional response to them was different from what their behaviour might suggest. Beneath the shouting and the chaos, I began to feel sadness and loneliness. This was someone who could have drunk alone in their room without bothering anyone, but loneliness, even if they didn't consciously recognize it, wouldn't let them. So, they went outside, just to be rejected, as the public ignored them, pedestrians walked past actively ignoring them, but when they pushed things far enough, the police would be called. And suddenly, they were no longer invisible. They were talking to someone, being acknowledged.

When managing homelessness services, I often had to intervene in situations like this. When paramedics, my staff, or police arrived, the first step was always to assess whether they had taken any drugs, to understand the risk they were facing and determine if they could be left alone safely, or if anything else was needed. If they were just drunk, the police or my staff would sometimes let them go, and they knew this. So many times, they wouldn't say if they had taken anything or not. They played with this uncertainty, and in doing so, they kept the interaction going. Suddenly, young police officers were engaging with them, being friendly, having a chat and for a moment, they weren't being ignored.

This is an example of how countertransference becomes invaluable. Tuning into my own emotional responses changed my perception. Instead of feeling irritated or defensive towards an "unruly alcoholic," I began to feel moved and saddened by them.

The key idea is how useful our own emotions can be in guiding us through the therapeutic experience. Our observations can only take us so far, but our intuition and emotional responses can take us deeper, helping us connect with parts of the experience that the patient themselves may be desperately avoiding. These emotional responses offer insight into the unspoken and often unconscious aspects of the patient's inner world, allowing us to engage with them in ways that facilitate deeper understanding and healing.

References

Abend, S. M. (2008). Unconscious Fantasy and Modern Conflict Theory. *Psychoanalytic Inquiry, 28*, 117–130.

Abram, J. (1996). *The Language of Winnicott: A Dictionary of Winnicott's Use of Words*. Karnac.

Abram, J. (2022). *The Surviving Object*. Routledge.

Abram, J., & Hinshelwood, R. D. (2018). *The Clinical Paradigms of Melanie Klein and Donald Winnicott*. Routledge.

Aggarwal, N. K. (2011). Intersubjectivity, Transference, and the Cultural Third. *Contemporary Psychoanalysis, 47*, 204–223.

Bailly, L. (2009). *Lacan: A Beginner's Guide*. Oneworld Publications.

Balint, M. (1979). *The Basic Fault: Therapeutic Aspects of Regression*. Brunner/Mazel.

Beauvoir, S. (1997). *The Second Sex*. Vintage.

Bollas, C. (1987). *The Shadow of the Object: Psychoanalysis of the Unthought Known*. Columbia University Press.

Bowlby, J. (1960). Separation Anxiety. *International Journal of Psychoanalysis, 41*, 89–113.

Bowlby, J. (1973). *Attachment and Loss: Vol. 2. Separation: Anger and Anxiety*. Pimlico.

Britton, R. (1989). The Oedipus Complex Today: Clinical Implications. In R. Britton, M. Feldman, & E. O'Shaughnessy (Eds.), *The Oedipus Complex Today* (pp. 89–113). Karnac.

Bromberg, P. M. (1993). Discussion. *Contemporary Psychoanalysis, 29*, 90–100.

Bronstein, C. (Ed.). (2001). *Kleinian Theory: A Contemporary Perspective*. Wiley.

Caldwell, L., & Joyce, A. (2011). *Reading Winnicott*. Routledge.

Caldwell, L., & Joyce, A. (2014). Essentially Winnicott: Creating Psychic Health. *British Journal of Psychotherapy, 30*, 18–32.

Cozolino, L. (2014). *The Neuroscience of Human Relationships: Attachment and the Developing Social Brain* (2nd ed.). W.W. Norton & Company.

Curtis, M. (Director). (1942). *Casablanca* [Film]. Warner Bros.

Dalal, F. (2015). Prejudice as Ideology: The Creation of "Us" and "Them" Groups in Society (and Psychoanalysis). *Psychotherapy and Politics International, 13*(3), 182–193.

Damasio, A. (2010). *Self Comes to Mind*. Vintage Books.

Davids, M. F. (2011). *Internal Racism: A Psychoanalytic Approach to Race and Difference*. Palgrave Macmillan.

Deleuze, G., & Guattari, F. (1972). *Anti-Oedipus: Capitalism and Schizophrenia*. University of Minnesota Press.

Escandon, R. S. (2023). A Reflection on Self-Disclosure. *British Journal of Psychotherapy, 39*, 765–780.

Fonagy, P. (2014). On Individual Psychotherapy and the Science of Psychodynamics by David Malan. *British Journal of Psychiatry, 204*(4), 282.
Freud, S. (1896). Further Remarks on the Neuro-Psychoses of Defence. *The Standard Edition of the Complete Psychological Works of Sigmund Freud, 3*, 157–185.
Freud, S. (1899). Screen Memories. *The Standard Edition of the Complete Psychological Works of Sigmund Freud, 3*, 299–322.
Freud, S. (1900). The Interpretation of Dreams. *The Standard Edition of the Complete Psychological Works of Sigmund Freud, 4*, ix–627.
Freud, S. (1912). Recommendations to Physicians Practising Psycho-Analysis. *The Standard Edition of the Complete Psychological Works of Sigmund Freud, 12*, 109–120.
Freud, S. (1913). Totem and Taboo: Some Points of Agreement between the Mental Lives of Savages and Neurotics (1913 [1912–13]). *The Standard Edition of the Complete Psychological Works of Sigmund Freud, 13*, vii–162.
Freud, S. (1914). On Narcissism: An Introduction. *The Standard Edition of the Complete Psychological Works of Sigmund Freud, 14*, 67–102.
Freud, S. (1915). The Unconscious. *The Standard Edition of the Complete Psychological Works of Sigmund Freud, 14*, 159–215.
Freud, S. (1917). Mourning and Melancholia. *The Standard Edition of the Complete Psychological Works of Sigmund Freud, 14*, 237–258.
Freud S (1918). From the History of an Infantile Neurosis. *SE, 17*, 1–124.
Freud, S. (1921). Group Psychology and the Analysis of the Ego. *The Standard Edition of the Complete Psychological Works of Sigmund Freud, 18*, 65–144.
Freud, S. (1923). The Ego and the Id. *The Standard Edition of the Complete Psychological Works of Sigmund Freud, 19*, 1–66.
Freud, S. (1927a). Inhibition, Symptom and Anxiety—An Abstract. *Psychoanalytic Review, 14*, 207–228.
Freud, S. (1927b). The Future of an Illusion. *The Standard Edition of the Complete Psychological Works of Sigmund Freud, 21*, 1–56.
Freud, S. (1933). New Introductory Lectures on Psycho-Analysis. *The Standard Edition of the Complete Psychological Works of Sigmund Freud, 22*, 1–182.
Freud, A. (1987). *The Writings of Anna Freud: The Ego and the Mechanisms of Defense*. International Universities Press.
Gomez, L. (1997). *An Introduction to Object Relations*. Free Association Books.
Hinshelwood, R. D. (2013). *Research on the Couch: Single-Case Studies, Subjectivity and Psychoanalytic Knowledge*. Routledge.
Horney, K. (1933). The Denial of the Vagina—A Contribution to the Problem of the Genital Anxieties Specific to Women. *International Journal of Psychoanalysis, 14*, 57–70.
Kernberg, O. (Ed.). (2004). *Contemporary Controversies in Psychoanalytic Theory, Techniques, and Their Applications*. American Psychiatric Publishing.

Kernberg, O. (2006). Psychoanalytic Affect Theory in the Light of Contemporary Neurobiological Findings. In E. Zacharacopoulou (Ed.), *Beyond the Mind-Body Dualism: Psychoanalysis and the Human Body* (Vol. 1286, pp. 106–117). Elsevier Health Sciences.

Kernberg, O. F. (2015). Neurobiological Correlates of Object Relations Theory: The Relationship Between Neurobiological and Psychodynamic Development. *International Forum of Psychoanalysis, 24*, 38–46.

Kernberg, O. F. (2021). Some Implications of New Developments in Neurobiology for Psychoanalytic Object Relations Theory. *Journal of the American Psychoanalytic Association, 48*(4), 1055–1081.

King, P. (1978). Affective Response of the Analyst to the Patient's Communications. *International Journal of Psychoanalysis, 59*, 329–334.

Klein, M. (1928). Early Stages of the Oedipus Conflict. *International Journal of Psychoanalysis, 9*, 167–180.

Klein, M. (1935). A Contribution to the Psychogenesis of Manic-Depressive States. *International Journal of Psychoanalysis, 16*, 145–174.

Klein, M. (1945). The Oedipus Complex in the Light of Early Anxieties. *International Journal of Psychoanalysis, 26*, 11–33.

Klein, M. (1946). Notes on Some Schizoid Mechanisms. *International Journal of Psychoanalysis, 27*, 99–110.

Kohon, G. (1984). Reflections on Dora: The Case of Hysteria. *International Journal of Psychoanalysis, 65*, 73–84.

Lacan, J. (1951). La etapa del espejo, fuente de la función del Yo a la luz de la experiencia psicoanalítica. *Revista de Psicoanálisis (REVAPA), 8*, 281–282.

Lemma, A. (2003). *Introduction to the Practice of Psychoanalytic Psychotherapy*. Wiley.

Lemma, A. (2016). *Introduction to the Practice of Psychoanalytic Psychotherapy* (2nd ed.). Wiley-Blackwell.

Little, M. (1951). Countertransference and the Patient's Response to It. *International Journal of Psychoanalysis, 32*, 32–40.

Malan, D. H. (1979). *Individual Psychotherapy and the Science of Psychodynamics*. Elsevier.

Mitchell, S. A., & Black, M. J. (1995). *Freud and Beyond: A History of Modern Psychoanalytic Thought*. Basic Books.

Ogden, T. H. (1992). Comments on Transference and Countertransference in the Initial Analytic Meeting. *Psychoanalytic Inquiry, 12*, 225–247.

Ogden, T. H. (2012). *Freud's "Mourning and Melancholia" and the Origins of Object Relations Theory*. https://doi.org/10.4324/9780203125298-2

Rangell, L. (1988). Roots and Derivatives of Unconscious Fantasy. In H. Blum et al. (Eds.), *Fantasy, Myth and Reality* (pp. 1–22). International Universities Press.

Rohleder, P., & Abrahams, D. (2020). *Clinical Guide to Psychodynamic Psychotherapy*. CRC Press.

Rosenfeld, H. (1964). On the Psychopathology of Narcissism: A Clinical Approach. *The International Journal of Psycho-Analysis, 45*, 332–337.
Roth, P. (2001). The Paranoid-Schizoid Position. In C. Bronstein (Ed.), *Kleinian Theory: A Contemporary Perspective* (pp. 32–46). Whurr Publishers.
Sandler, J. (1976). Countertransference and Role-Responsiveness. *The International Journal of Psychoanalysis, 53*, 43–47.
Shatz, C. (1990). Impulse Activity and the Patterning of Connections During CNS Development. *Neuron, 5*(6), 745–756.
Shatz, C. J. (1992). The prenatal development of the visual system. In M. J. Chalupa & W. Rhoades (Eds.), *Development and organization of the retina: From molecules to function* (pp. 21–50). Springer.
Steiner, J. (1987). The Interplay Between Pathological Organizations and the Paranoid-Schizoid and Depressive Positions. *The International Journal of Psychoanalysis, 68*, 69–80.
Steiner, J. (1993). *Psychic Retreats: Pathological Organizations in Psychotic, Neurotic and Borderline Patients*. Routledge.
Winnicott, D. W. (1970). Cure. In *Home Is Where We Start From: Essays by a Psychoanalyst* (pp. 112–122). Norton.
Winnicott, D. W. (1971). *Playing and Reality*. Tavistock Publications.
Winnicott, D. W. (1974). Fear of Breakdown. *International Review of Psychoanalysis, 1*, 103–107.
Žižek, S. (2018). *Like a Thief in Broad Daylight*. Penguin.

CHAPTER 3

Assessment and Suitability

Introduction

One of the key challenges in clinical practice is determining the most appropriate therapeutic approach for a patient. While psychodynamic and psychoanalytic therapies offer deep exploration and transformation, they require a certain level of psychological capacity, consistency, and commitment, factors that not all patients can meet.

Psychoanalysis, as Coltart (1986) noted, is only suitable for a small percentage of patients, particularly those who can engage in intensive treatment at a frequency of four to five sessions per week. Even psychodynamic therapy, when reduced to a once-a-week format, presents difficulties, as the therapeutic process unfolds at a much slower pace, limiting the depth of exploration. Patients seen once weekly may have approximately 25 sessions in six months, whereas those in psychoanalysis receive over 100 in the same timeframe. This difference profoundly affects the role of therapy in a patient's life, the continuity of the work, and what can be processed within the therapeutic relationship.

Supportive therapy becomes a more suitable option when a patient either cannot commit to long-term, high-frequency treatment or lacks the psychological capacity for sustained exploration. Some patients struggle to think about their emotions in a way that makes deep interpretation useful for them, exploratory interventions may feel confusing, destabilizing, or

R. S. Escandon, *Contemporary Developments in Supportive Therapy*, Palgrave Texts in Counselling and Psychotherapy,
https://doi.org/10.1007/978-3-031-96059-8_3

simply irrelevant. Others may be unable to sustain a therapeutic process over years due to external constraints, such as financial limitations, service structures, or personal instability. In these cases, supportive therapy, rooted in psychoanalytic understanding but adapted to the patient's needs, provides a more realistic and effective intervention.

The following section explores how to assess whether a patient is best suited for supportive therapy and how to structure an assessment process that can determine this effectively.

Diagnosis vs/and Formulation

Diagnosis is typically understood as the process of identifying a set of characteristics, usually symptoms, that correlate with a particular disorder, as outlined in mental health manuals such as the DSM-5. This is usually followed by a standardized treatment recommendation. Formulation, on the other hand, offers a more individualized and comprehensive understanding of a patient's psychological functioning, focusing on unconscious dynamics, developmental history, ego functioning, defences, and patterns of attachment or relating.

The role of the assessor is undeniably challenging, as they must discern psychological patterns that may only become fully apparent after months of therapy within a brief assessment period. Some, like Kernberg (1984b, 2019b), focus on identifying traits that align the patient with specific personality structures, while others, such as Hinshelwood (1991), Coltart (1986), and Malan (1976), aim to capture the patient's unconscious way of relating. Regardless of the approach, a thorough understanding of the patient's background, needs, and circumstances is essential before beginning any form of therapeutic intervention.

As Hinshelwood (1991) describes, formulation is preferred over diagnosis because it provides a deeper, more individualized perspective, one that moves beyond classification to meaningfully inform the therapeutic process. This does not necessarily mean that psychoanalysis is opposed to diagnostic manuals, it simply prioritizes a deeper understanding of unconscious relational patterns over a generalized diagnostic label, which may not fully capture the individual's experience.

The nature of some patients' circumstances may necessitate a multidisciplinary approach, which can only be effectively coordinated through a diagnostic framework. For example, if a patient with a schizoaffective disorder experiences a life-changing accident and seeks supportive therapy, the practitioner must be prepared to address the complex interplay between their psychiatric condition and their current situation. Understanding how schizoaffective disorder affects the patient's daily life, treatment needs, and general well-being is crucial. In such cases, collaboration with a psychiatrist or home treatment team may be required; these doors will only be accessed with a diagnosis. In this section we will not explore how to diagnose, so therapists who are not clinical psychologists or psychiatrists may need to refer patients for an alternative assessment, one that prioritizes diagnosis over determining therapeutic suitability.

Another aspect to consider, besides formulation and potential role of a diagnosis, is the therapeutic relationship. The relationship begins the moment the patient makes contact, whether through an initial inquiry or when they enter the consultant's office. The atmosphere of the first interview is crucial in establishing a strong therapeutic foundation.

The assessment phase of a supportive intervention initiates when the patient is invited to a semi-structured interview with a dual purpose: to collect essential information that will be used to make a formulation and to provide sympathetic listening. A skilled assessor knows not only how to ask pertinent questions but also what not to ask, drawing insights from both what the patient expresses and what they omit (Mackinnon et al., 2016). Using a structured questionnaire during the assessment may send the wrong message, making the process feel overly medical or clinical. Instead, it is often more effective for the assessor to hold in mind the key areas that need to be covered rather than relying on a form. Allowing the patient to speak freely often provides most of the necessary information without requiring excessive direct questioning.

A comprehensive assessment should explore the following three areas:

1. Patient suitability—Assessing the individual's needs, psychological capacity, and potential responsiveness to supportive therapy
2. External support (multidisciplinary approach)—Identifying whether additional professional involvement (e.g. psychiatrists, social workers, medical teams) is necessary and the role each professional has in the care of the patient and in case of emergency
3. Therapist competency—Ensuring the practitioner has the necessary skills and knowledge to provide effective supportive intervention for the specific case

Assessment Process

A good referral should already have sufficient information about the patient's history. When possible, it is ideal to have a conversation with the person who referred the patient (Coltart, 1986). However, in my experience, thorough assessments where professionals take their time to know a person, gather their history, and write detailed notes are rare. In such cases, or when there is no referral and you are the first mental health professional to see the patient, it may be helpful to use a questionnaire sent to the patient before the initial consultation or ensure there is time during the initial consultation to review all the key areas.

When meeting with the patient, it is best to avoid starting with too narrow a focus: a psychoanalytically informed, semi-structured interview is preferred. If there are some specific areas to explore, these can be referred to a speciality if the therapist is working in the NHS. This broader perspective helps the therapist gain a comprehensive understanding of the patient's inner world and the nature of their distress within the limited time available. This approach not only helps determine their suitability for psychotherapy but also provides valuable insights into the patient as an individual (Milton, 1997). It builds a sense of who they are and how it will feel being with them and working with them. It is important to understand that if the therapist does start with a supportive intervention, the therapeutic alliance has already begun, and how the therapist attends to this early interaction could be the difference between a successful treatment and a failing one.

There is no single way to begin relating to a patient, but it is essential that the assessment sessions remain patient-focused. Some therapists, eager to build a good relationship, act out of anxiety—interrupting, failing to really be present for the patient, or becoming preoccupied with completing a questionnaire or gathering information instead of observing their patients and the impact the therapist attitude is having on them. This is not an ideal way to start therapy, and if the expectation is that once the assessment is over, the therapist will suddenly start relating with the patient differently; this will be confusing for the patient. It is a complex balance between gathering information and making space for the patient. Consider the following cases.

I once managed a complaint from a patient, who was a police officer struggling with the emotional toll of her job. She wanted to establish a clear boundary between work and home life so that she wouldn't constantly think about work when with her family. In her first therapy session, she didn't know what to say, and the silence became unsettling for the therapist, who felt responsible for her not talking. Out of anxiety, the therapist asked whether she had seen a popular police TV show, commenting on how good it was. Here, we can see a disconnect: the therapist believed they were building rapport by finding common ground, while the patient felt misunderstood, she had come to therapy hoping to detach from her work, not engage with it further.

A different case involved a patient who sought therapy due to persistent sadness. The treatment took place via Zoom. During the first two sessions, the patient remained mostly silent, and at some point, she was completely silent for more than 30 minutes, and what she was saying was brief, not really giving me much room to intervene, so I remained quiet but present. In the third session, she shared how difficult it was for her to talk about her emotions and how much courage it takes to speak. She expressed relief that I had not pressured her to talk. Though this case occurred after an initial assessment, it illustrates the importance of following the patient's agenda, not our own. It is easy to feel that is our job to make the patient talk, and it is easy to understand the first therapist's attempt to make her feel comfortable and help her start talking, but that is not the stand we have. If the patient can't talk, we need to reflect why that is the case. We can ask some questions or make some comments, but ultimately ensure the space is one for the patients.

I recommend offering two assessment sessions, when possible, scheduled at least a week apart, and clearly communicating to the patient that these sessions are for assessment purposes only. This is just in case the therapist doesn't consider supportive interventions suitable and they then need to refer. It is therefore crucial that the patient understands this is not the start of therapy, but rather a period for gathering information and determining the best course of action.

At the end of the second session, the therapist should allow time for the patient to ask practical questions and for them to clarify any points from the questionnaire or referral. Before making a decision, the therapist should have a comprehensive mental health history. It is poor practice to accept a patient and begin fostering a sense of safety and reliability, only for the treatment to collapse later because the case became too high-risk; something that could have been predicted with a more thorough assessment.

The patient should also feel free to seek another therapist if they do not feel comfortable with the current therapist. At this early stage, if a patient is unhappy with the therapist's approach, fees, or location, it may not be an unconscious projection but a genuine concern that should be addressed. A common example is when a woman who has experienced sexual abuse seeks therapy with a male therapist. While there is potential therapeutic value in working with a male therapist to explore and rebuild trust, this is not always the patient's immediate focus. If her primary concern is, for instance, work-related difficulties, she may not wish to revisit past trauma at this stage. In such cases, if after the assessment, these concerns come up, a referral to a female therapist might be the most appropriate option.

Patient Suitability

The assessment should include identifying the reason for consultation, exploring family and developmental history, evaluating mental health history, understanding previous therapeutic experiences, conducting risk assessments, and addressing other relevant subjects that help build a formulation of the patient. This includes relationship history, work experience, and more. Individuals with severe personality disorders, mood disorders, psychosis, substance misuse, and history of PTSD may require more specialized interventions. However, these need not necessarily be exclusion criteria, in certain cases. Particularly when there is a multidisciplinary team in place, supportive intervention can be utilized and become a better option than traditional therapy. (I will expand on this in the following section.)

Before starting the assessment, two criteria of exclusion should be kept in mind. If one of both applies, this suggests that a full assessment might not be necessary:

1. *Assessment for Trauma*. It is crucial to determine if the individual has recently experienced a severe traumatic event and is presenting symptoms of PTSD. In such cases, trauma-focused therapy may be more appropriate. There is an important distinction between patients who *have* suffered from PTSD from patients who are *currently* suffering from it. Supportive therapy is only suitable for patients who *have* suffered PTSD, but in the present time have no active symptoms.

Similarly, individuals dealing with anxiety disorders resulting from recent crises, such as recurrent panic attacks, night terrors, or avoidant behaviour, might benefit more from interventions such as Cognitive Behavioural Therapy (CBT).

Supportive therapy may not be suitable in cases where symptoms require immediate intervention before the patient can effectively engage in talking therapy. Discussing the area in which they need support might initially worsen their condition. Here are two examples of this.

A patient came to see me after experiencing bereavement and subsequently developed an anxiety disorder. They began having panic attacks at work, accompanied by uncontrollable shaking. To make matters worse, they worked as a hairdresser, meaning that their symptoms directly interfered with their ability to perform their job.

During our sessions, whenever they recalled memories of the person they had lost, without any exploration on my part, their panic attacks intensified, making it impossible for them to continue working. While I believe that supportive therapy could have been beneficial once their symptoms were more manageable, at this stage the process was doing more harm than good. The recommendation was CBT to help the patient regain a sense of control over their symptoms and restore aspects of their daily life.

A similar case I supervised involved a police officer who had experienced a traumatic incident at work. After just a few sessions, she wanted to stop therapy because talking about the event was making her feel worse. They began experiencing night terrors and started drinking after sessions to cope. In this case, I recommended re-referring the patient for Eye Movement Desensitization and Reprocessing (EMDR), as it could provide a more structured and trauma-focused approach.

It is crucial not to proceed with the assessment if a patient exhibits these kinds of reactions. For some individuals, telling their story too soon can be retraumatizing. If a referral to a trauma clinic is necessary, there is no need for the patient to recount everything to a therapist they will not continue working with. Additionally, the clinic will likely conduct its own assessment, making a premature in-depth discussion unnecessary and potentially harmful.

2. *Motivation.* Evaluating a patient's motivation is crucial. For individuals who lack motivation and have been referred by someone else, it may be more beneficial to leave the option open for them to return when they are ready, rather than starting therapy prematurely.

Authors such as Lester Luborsky (1984), Luborsky et al. (1990) and Otto Kernberg (1984a, 2019a) have consistently emphasized that a patient's willingness to engage is essential for therapy to be effective. If a person is sent to therapy by a relative or a probation officer and does not wish to attend, offering treatment may be futile. It is also misleading to suggest that therapy can succeed without the patient's motivation. However, if the patient is ambivalent, angry, devaluing the process before it begins, or uncertain about needing help, therapy can still proceed, and these emotions will be part of the early work.

These two factors motivation and symptomatology can often be screened over the phone without the need to book a full assessment. This process is commonly referred to as a telephone consultation.

Suitability for Treatment

To determine suitability, the focus should be on creating a formulation that can answer three critical questions. Is it safe? Is it the best option? Will it be beneficial? To answer these, the following aspects should be thoroughly reviewed during the two assessment sessions before accepting a patient:

- Identifying the reason for consultation
- Identifying the latent motive for therapy, referring to the underlying unconscious reasons for seeking therapeutic help (Shedler, 2010)
- Evaluating the patient's mental health history (diagnosis, treatments, historical and current outcomes)
- Understanding previous therapeutic experiences
- Exploring family and developmental history
- Exploring emotional intelligence
  - Gaining insight into their difficulties
  - Assessing their ability to reflect on thoughts and emotions
  - Assessing their capacity to relate to others without resorting to splitting
  - Evaluating their capacity to maintain relationships
  - Evaluating their ability to address conflict without jeopardizing relationships
- Exploring their level of psychological flexibility:
  - Capacity to adapt to change

  - Capacity to manage difficult emotions without becoming overwhelmed
  - Ability to tolerate different perspectives
- Gaining an early sense of transference and countertransference
- Conducting a risk assessment:
  - Substance misuse
  - History of harm to themselves or others (forensic history if relevant)
  - History of domestic abuse
  - Potential risk to dependents (only if relevant)
- Medical history. (If there is a medical condition this may have an emotional impact. There is no need for too many details.)
- Addressing other subjects relevant to their current mental health support, such as their relationship with other practitioners

There are no universal rules for how to ask about these elements, or what is and isn't pertinent. The key is to remain emotionally attuned to the patient from the beginning, rather than succumbing to the pressure of conducting an intensive exploration in an attempt to complete the assessment. For example, if a patient is struggling to discuss a traumatic event, there is no need for the assessor to gather specific details if the event does not pose a serious risk or constitute a reason to recommend a different intervention. In such cases, the assessor can simply move on.

Conversely, if the patient is eager to discuss an important aspect of their life, the assessor should allow them to speak freely. It may be best to schedule an additional session, if necessary, rather than stopping them from sharing something significant that they may not have disclosed to anyone before. From the beginning, having a supportive stance is important. If the therapist makes the patient feel that what they are saying is not important, this will have an impact when the therapy starts.

We can artificially subdivide each point to answer these questions and create a formulation. For example:

Is it safe?

- Conducting a risk assessment:
  - Substance misuse
  - History of harm to themselves or others (forensic history if relevant)
  - History of domestic abuse
  - Potential risk to dependents (only if relevant)

Is it the best option?

- Identifying the reason for consultation
- Identifying the latent motive for therapy, referring to the underlying unconscious reasons for seeking therapeutic help (Shedler, 2010)
- Evaluating the patient's mental health history (diagnosis, treatments, historical and current outcomes)

Will it be beneficial?

- Exploring emotional intelligence
  - Gaining insight into their difficulties
  - Assessing their ability to reflect on thoughts and emotions
  - Assessing their capacity to relate to others without resorting to splitting
  - Evaluating their capacity to maintain relationships
  - Evaluating their ability to address conflict without jeopardizing relationships
- Exploring their level of psychological flexibility
  - Capacity to adapt to change
  - Capacity to manage difficult emotions without becoming overwhelmed
  - Ability to tolerate different perspectives
- Understanding previous therapeutic experiences
- Exploring family and developmental history
- Gaining an early sense of transference and countertransference
- Medical history
- Addressing other subjects relevant to their current mental health support, such as his relationship with other practitioners

Evaluate the Risk, Expectations, and Capacity to Tolerate a Therapeutic Process

The therapist should assess the risk always in relation to the support available to the patient and address the expectation for example:

Example 1: Patients' Expectations and Capacity to Use Therapy

A man in his mid-30s recently lost his job, and soon after, his boyfriend ended their relationship, saying the patient had become too angry and difficult to be around. Overwhelmed by distress, the patient struggled for a while but has now found a new job and is beginning to regain some stability. He isn't sure what he wants from therapy but knows he doesn't want to explore his anger or underlying issues. Instead, he seeks a space to talk and process his emotions. During the assessment, it becomes clear that he has low emotional intelligence (he struggled to see the relation between his emotions and life events for example) and limited psychological flexibility (he couldn't listen to others' views), struggles to maintain relationships, and tends to split. Furthermore, when faced with disagreement, he becomes highly emotional, and there is a past incident where he acted violently by throwing objects. Given these factors, the therapist believes he would struggle with exploratory work at this time but acknowledges his need for support. In this case, supportive therapy would be a suitable approach.

This is an example of a case where a psychodynamic psychotherapist might offer treatment at a frequency of once per week. Initially, interventions would be minimal, but over time, the therapist would attempt to engage with the patient's "resistance" or "defences" potentially leading to conflict with the therapist and a high likelihood of dropout.

It can be tempting to push for exploration or resolution, but if the patient is not ready or seeking that, the expectation is to feel better. In this case, the patient may primarily need a period of stability, allowing their defences to regain strength after a difficult time. If the therapist imposes an agenda that does not align with this need, it risks creating a mismatch that could hinder the therapeutic process. I have seen many therapists blame the patient's resistance when this happened, when it was clear from the beginning that the patient was going to be resistant towards treatment.

Example 2: Patient Risk and Multidisciplinary Team

Another example is a patient in her early 30s who has a diagnosis of bipolar disorder. She experiences severe manic episodes, becoming impulsive and struggling to keep her job and social commitments. These periods can include anger and possible violence, followed by depressive episodes lasting a few months, where she becomes suicidal. She is tired of what she calls "classic therapy." She didn't find it useful and simply wants someone to listen to her and hear what she is going through, not trying to cure her or talk about her episodes and medication: someone to be there for her until she discovers what she wants in life and what she can achieve despite her disorder.

She has a multidisciplinary team, including a psychiatrist and a home treatment team that can send a psychiatric nurse to her house when needed. The therapist sees her in a hospital setting, in a secondary care unit, ensuring she has the specialized support required to manage her symptoms safely. She will be suitable for supportive intervention, although without these teams, it would not be safe to work with her in a private setting. Her expectations are also aligned with those of supportive therapy.

For challenging patients, like the first example, supportive intervention can be a gentler approach. It is a good alternative for patients who may lack what Britton (2003) called the *triangular space*, the capacity to hold a third position that allows differentiation between subjective and objective reality (as discussed in Chap. 2). This space facilitates self-reflection and empathy by integrating the self, the other, and an observing third, which is crucial for thinking about relationships and accepting differing viewpoints.

A patient who becomes violent when confronted with opposing opinions, like the example above, exemplifies someone who may struggle with traditional psychodynamic therapy.

Britton (2005) discusses a case in which a patient reacted with violent rage when presented with an alternative perspective, highlighting the difficulty some individuals have in maintaining an independent mind without experiencing different viewpoints as a threat. Britton, one of the most skilled clinicians, managed to work with such patients within an intensive setting, multiple sessions per week over an extended period. However, not all therapists can provide this level of treatment, nor do all clinical settings allow for such long-term, high-frequency work.

For these patients, supportive therapy offers a more suitable approach by emphasizing containment and stability rather than confrontation and deep exploration. It provides a structured space that fosters emotional regulation without overwhelming the patient.

Another group of patients well-suited for supportive therapy includes those Rosenfeld (1987) described as having *thin-skinned narcissism* and those Alessandra Lemma (2009) referred to as relating through a *one-way mirror* mother. These individuals tend to be highly vulnerable, hypervigilant, and easily humiliated, often leaving therapists feeling as though they are "walking on eggshells." Such patients struggle to tolerate the intensity of psychodynamic psychotherapy, particularly when they misinterpret interpretations as personal criticisms rather than invitations to think. A gentler therapeutic approach can help prevent early dropout.

Many therapists begin psychodynamic treatment with these patients, only to encounter premature termination. Bateman (1998) noted that individuals with thick-skinned narcissism often struggle to stay in therapy, finding breaks difficult and rejecting interventions that imply dependency, as they maintain an impenetrable sense of superiority. In contrast, those with thin-skinned narcissism, as described by Diamond et al. (2021), fluctuate between vulnerability and an appearance of strength, often responding to interventions with shame, rejection, or feelings of humiliation. These oscillations frequently lead to abrupt termination. Even well-crafted and accurate interpretations may not prevent this outcome.

In both cases, when their sense of superiority or self-image is threatened, these patients are prone to breakdowns. As Diamond et al. (2021), Bateman (1998), and Rosenfeld (1987) suggest, classic psychodynamic methods may not be effective. They advocate for modifications to the therapeutic approach, such as avoiding excessive neutrality and minimizing negative transference: principles that align closely with supportive therapy. These are the characteristics that the assessor needs to keep in mind when making a recommendation.

By prioritizing the therapeutic alliance and reducing the risk of dropout, supportive therapy provides a more accessible and stabilizing intervention for patients who might otherwise struggle in more exploratory treatments. As mentioned, the number of sessions also becomes extremely relevant. If a patient disagrees with an intervention a therapist made on a Monday but sees them again on Wednesday and then again on Friday, for example, then they have plenty of time to address this. In the case of once a week therapy, the patient might be left feeling distressed for a full week. In some cases the patient might find the process too challenging and may leave.

Assessing these patients can be difficult, as their presentation may not always be consistent. However, if their history reveals repeated instances of feeling hurt by family members or friends, leading to feelings of vulnerability, weakness, and humiliation rather than sadness, it is likely that they will struggle with interpretive techniques. They might take an interpretation or observation as an insult rather than something to consider. A trainee shared with me a case where, after a long and friendly assessment, he told the patient that the NHS waiting time was above a year. The patient left in rage, after insulting the trainee and making severe accusations. The patient was extremely sensitive to these far from ideal circumstances. This helps us understand the struggles of communicating with such patients, and using such complex tools like interpretations that are so easily misinterpreted.

I often introduce a brief, gentle interpretation during the assessment: one that presents the patient with an idea they haven't considered before. This can be a valuable indicator of their capacity for self-reflection. When patients struggle in this area, they often react with irritation, immediately seeking to defensively explain why I am wrong. Rather than considering the perspective as one of many possible viewpoints, they treat it as a challenge to be refuted.

In the cases described, supportive therapy is the better recommendation as it helps patients during difficult times and is not focusing on cure, problem-solving, strategies, or other techniques. Also, if the therapist is not able to offer more sessions in a week, the idea of exploratory work with them becomes even less possible.

Later, when patients feel better, they might seek something more exploratory, and a referral can be made for either psychoanalysis or psychodynamic therapy. For example, the patient, above, might later want to explore his anger, and other components of his life, and would be able to tolerate rather better the different opinions of the therapist. In all probability, having had a first positive, supportive therapeutic experience, this will facilitate the beginning of something more exploratory later.

Assessing Risk: Suicide

The therapist may not always need to explore suicidal risk in depth, but when there is a history of previous attempts or active ideation, it is crucial that this be assessed thoroughly during the evaluation. It is also important not to make assumptions; suicidal thoughts must be directly addressed, whether through a questionnaire, a screening tool, or during the interview.

When evaluating suicide risk, a comprehensive assessment should consider various factors, including developmental history, coping abilities, and recent triggers (The Erikson Institute of the Austen Riggs Center, 2018):

- Understanding a patient's developmental and family history is crucial when assessing suicide risk. Past traumas, losses, and disruptions in attachment can impact their reliance on external support for self-esteem maintenance. A family history of suicide is particularly significant, as individuals with relatives who have died by suicide are at a higher risk themselves (Qin et al., 2002). Additionally, the therapist should explore how the patient perceives their upbringing and familial relationships. For example, a patient who views their entire family history as solely negative, unable to acknowledge any positive figures, may be at higher risk than someone who, despite experiencing depression, sees their family as an ongoing source of support.

- *Triggering Events.* Identifying recent stressors and evaluating their impact on the patient's stability is crucial. It's important to understand what specifically triggers distress for the patient, beyond just the dates or external events. For example, in a case I worked with, the anniversary of a daughter's death was a powerful trigger, leading to two serious suicide attempts on that date. Similarly, a patient who attempted suicide after a breakup may not be distressed by the date itself or the ongoing relationship with their ex-partner, but rather by their intense emotional reaction to later rejections. Understanding the patient's emotional vulnerabilities and how they process these events is key to assessing risk.
- *External Support.* Assessing the quality of relationships and social roles, not only—as mentioned—with their families but also with friends and professionals who are working with them. If they are working with an HTT (home treatment team), it is important to have a sense of their relationship, as this can determine if they will contact them during a crisis or not.
- *Aggression and Self-Directed Behaviour.* Evaluating the presence and direction of aggression is crucial in assessing the risk of self-harm and suicidal ideation. This aggression may manifest as direct physical harm to the body or indirectly through self-sabotaging behaviours in relationships and professional life. For example, I recall a case in which a patient deliberately humiliated himself in a public setting, leading his friends to distance themselves from him. This was not the first time he had done it, and when exploring this, he expressed how much hate he felt for himself when people thought he was a respectful person. This act significantly increased his sadness and placed him at a higher risk.
- *Emotional Regulation and Protective Factors.* Assessing a patient's ability to manage intense negative emotions and identifying protective factors that reduce their risk of self-harm. Some individuals cope

with distress by engaging in healthy activities such as exercise, meeting a friend for coffee, focusing on work, or pursuing hobbies. Others, however, may turn to substance use, impulsive sexual encounters they later regret, or complete withdrawal—staying in bed and isolating themselves. Understanding how a patient responds to emotional distress is critical in assessing their overall risk and guiding appropriate therapeutic interventions. If a patient isolates from everyone when he or she is depressed, this will likely include the therapist if there is no HTT involved.

- *Reasons for Living*. Understanding what motivates the patient to continue living is crucial. A higher risk is present when the patient doesn't seem to have a clear motive for staying alive. I commonly hear people say, "I would never do this to my kids," meaning they will not attempt suicide because of the impact it would have on their children, reflecting a relationship they feel a strong need to protect and care for. Studies have shown that not having a reason for staying alive increases the presence of suicidal ideation during a suicide crisis (Brüdern et al., 2018).
- *Specific Risk Factors*. Open discussions about suicide plans, access to means, and potential triggers help clarify the severity of risk. There is higher risk when a patient has a plan than when the patient has ideation. For example, when a patient says they want to hang themselves, and they already bought a rope. This shows intent even if they are not immediately planning on acting on this.

These factors do not necessarily disqualify a patient from Supportive Therapy. However, before proceeding, the therapist must ensure that appropriate multidisciplinary teams are in place to work with the patient safely and effectively.

A high-risk patient with strong multidisciplinary support is often easier to work with than a low-risk patient in a private setting with no support beyond the therapist. Risk should always be assessed in relation to the available support systems. Additionally, it is important to consider whether these systems are already in place or if the patient is still waiting for a referral. In the NHS, referrals can take months, and there is no guarantee that a patient will be accepted into a team. It is always best to begin treatment once these support structures are established.

The sad reality is that even after careful assessment, suicide remains extremely difficult to predict. A study by the American Psychological

Association (2016) examined whether our ability to predict suicide had improved over the past 50 years, given extensive research on the subject. The findings showed no significant improvement; suicide remains highly unpredictable. However, this does not mean clinicians have no role to play. The characteristics described above can help identify when to intervene and build a clearer picture of the patient's struggles. While this may not allow for precise prediction of whether a patient will attempt suicide, it provides valuable insights for developing support plans and preventive measures. While some cases will always be unforeseeable, many are not, and it is in these situations that proactive assessment and intervention can make a crucial difference.

Reality Principle Assessment

Assessing the reality principle is crucial for distinguishing between psychotic and non-psychotic functioning (Kernberg, 2019b). This helps answer two key questions: Is the patient able to make use of supportive therapy? and Is it safe for them to start therapy, or do they need a different intervention?

There is no clear-cut answer to this. For example, volunteers in charities such as Hearing Voices are able to offer support to people who suffer from schizophrenia and other psychotic conditions. On the other hand, I recall working with homeless individuals where many psychotic conditions made even basic communication difficult. In such cases, there was no reasonable expectation that the person could engage meaningfully in any therapeutic process. This highlights the importance of assessing whether the patient's mental state allows for effective engagement in therapy, or if a different approach is required, and not just look at a diagnosis.

Reality Testing. This involves evaluating the patient's ability to differentiate between internal thoughts and external reality while maintaining empathy with social norms. From a psychodynamic perspective, impaired reality testing blurs the distinctions between the self and others, which complicates interpersonal interactions and the evaluation of reality (Kernberg, 2019a).

For example, I worked with a patient in the community who was convinced he was a space pilot, that babies came from Mars, and that everyone around him worked for the CIA. Whenever he felt anxious, he immediately believed someone from the CIA was spying on him. He would find evidence to support this belief, such as a white van parked in the road, a postman walking, a cleaner collecting bins, or even police officers just patrolling, all of whom he would consider secret agents. Even in his room, he would break electronics and examine small pieces he didn't understand, interpreting them as spy equipment. The key issue here was that his anxiety was not understood as a personal feeling, but rather something that was being done to him. This made it incredibly difficult to engage him in any meaningful conversation. Building a supportive relationship was impossible, as he would quickly turn anyone into a CIA agent, making therapy or even basic interaction unfeasible. The patient needs to be able to distinguish, at least to some degree, what are their personal struggles, so the support can be presented as something to address what they are going through, rather than as something that is being done to them.

On the other hand, there are patients with paranoid schizophrenia who can still engage with support, even when delusional, provided their delusions do not interfere with the interaction. I worked with another patient in the community who was convinced that if he didn't turn the heating to the maximum, snakes would come into his room. Despite his preoccupation with this fear, he was able to engage with staff and not involve them in his delusion. While his way of relating was certainly complex, he remained consistent and appreciative of the support people offered him, even when he was struggling. In such cases, supportive therapy may be more possible, though it still requires sensitivity and adaptability from the therapist.

Before initiating supportive therapy with a patient who struggles with reality testing at times, it is essential to ensure:

- *Patient Suitability.* Confirm that the patient's non-psychotic faculties are sufficiently intact to meaningfully engage in therapy. As the examples above.
- *Multidisciplinary Support.* A supportive team, including psychiatrists, crisis team, and home treatment specialists, is crucial for managing crises and ensuring therapeutic efficacy (discussed further in the section on external support).
- *Adaptability of Therapeutic Approach.* The therapist's expertise in adapting their approach is essential, including the willingness to adjust or abandon the analytic stance during crises. This flexibility ensures that the patient is supported effectively without compromising safety. A psychiatrist or psychiatric nurse who is also trained as a therapist is an example of someone capable of facilitating supportive

therapy while adjusting the approach when necessary (discussed further in the section on therapist competency).

By gathering this information, the therapist can assess whether the setting and their competencies are appropriate for the patient's needs. No therapist is suitable for every case; for instance, a therapist with trauma expertise may not be appropriate for working with forensic issues, substance misuse, psychosis, or certain personality disorders. (This will be discussed in the section about therapist competency.)

Evaluation of the Patient's Emotional Intelligence and Engagement Capacity to Determine Their Potential Benefit from Therapy

The patient's emotional capacity to feel either better or worse when speaking with the therapist during a session is a good indication of their emotional intelligence. It's common for patients to feel shy, struggle to express themselves, or feel exposed, but the key question is whether they can benefit from talking with others.

An example of this is when a patient does not understand the benefit of talking to someone. Their use of language may feel detached from emotional expression, as if conversation itself is not something that could help them, as if they lack an emotional dimension to reach or express feelings. For instance, during an assessment, a patient who was feeling anxious after his divorce asked me at the end of the assessment: "*How will talking about it make me feel better?*" This was an honest question. He recognized his anxiety and, to some extent, probably saw a connection to his divorce, but he genuinely could not understand how talking about it would change anything. During the assessment, although he could grasp why I was asking about his history and other aspects of his life, he remained unconvinced that speaking about his feelings could have any impact. I explained how therapy worked, and he couldn't understand why anyone would want to speak to someone that frequently.

At the same time, the emotional intelligence, as a capacity to feel, express, and understand emotional pain, is important. While working in an EAP (Employee Assistance Program) conducting assessments for police officers who had experienced trauma at work, it was common for them to say, "I can't do this… Sorry, I can't," when simply asked, "What brings you here?" Even though their difficulties were outlined in the questionnaire or referral, they were not in a place to talk about them.

In such cases, I often referred them to EMDR, where techniques like the window of tolerance could help them manage overwhelming emotions. This represents an extreme example of lacking ego capacity, where the patient is unable to emotional distress or engage in the process of narrating their own story.

Once the patient can allow open dialogue, understanding the patient's relational patterns (transference) and psychological mindedness is crucial in determining their capacity to benefit from therapy. Formulation around object relating should be considered. Hinshelwood (1991) emphasizes the continuity of internal object relationships across different aspects of a patient's life, past, present, and transference in terms of how they have engaged with the assessor. He highlights how internalized parental figures shape perception and interaction, influencing both the patient's experience of authority figures and their own parental role. The persistence of these internal dynamics, rather than just their origins, is central to psychotherapy. If a patient repeatedly finds themselves in the role of a victim during conflicts, frequently leaving relationships, or displaying other recurring patterns, this can provide valuable insight into the challenges that may arise in the therapeutic process.

For example, a supervisee once described a patient who, in the very first session, stated that her mother had abused her, her boyfriend had raped her, and no one had ever been there for her, concluding that the therapist should not expect her to trust her either. In this clear example, the patient's past experiences were presented as a definitive reason for their inability to trust. Soon after, the patient began missing sessions and arriving late, showing no interest in exploring these behaviours or their meaning within the therapy. This early dynamic signalled significant relational difficulties that would likely shape the course of treatment.

In contrast, if the patient can reflect on the motives for being late, or not attending, and they can consider the therapist's perspective (or interpretations) on their circumstances, they may benefit more from psychodynamic psychotherapy.

Something the assessor can use to explore the emotional capacity and determine suitability can be the following question written by Ciarrochi and Mayer (2007):

- *Perceiving Emotions.* Can the patient recognize their own feelings and understand others' emotions?
- *Using Emotions.* Can they express emotions to navigate problems?
- *Understanding Emotions.* Do they grasp the impact of their emotions and reactions?
- *Regulating Emotions.* Can they manage emotions constructively?
- *Emotions and Sociability.* Do their emotions foster or hinder relationships?

We can see the importance of the ego capacity to relate, to tolerate emotional pain, and to understand themselves, in making a recommendation. Limited emotional intelligence suggests that supportive therapy might be more appropriate, as it allows a more supportive stance. If the therapist prioritizes insight and interpretation when the patient cannot use them, therapy may be ineffective or even harmful. Additionally, psychodynamic or psychoanalytic interventions tend to be more successful when they last for several years and involve more than one session per week. A meta-analysis conducted by Falk Leichsenring and Sven Rabung (2011), which reviewed over 900 cases, concluded that very little benefit is found in short-term interventions (a few months long), at the same time psychodynamic therapy is effective when is provided for a longer period.

What this means is that if only one session per week can be offered, a psychodynamic approach may not be suitable, with an emotionally limited patient. It is important to remember that supportive interventions are not aimed at improving symptoms but at alleviating the patient's distress and providing consistent support. Offering psychodynamic therapy in such cases, which may increase distress and risk dropout, would not be advisable.

Many experienced psychodynamic therapists in such circumstances, when the patient can't use interpretations, tend not to interpret or push too much, as they understand timing is not right. However, that is the point of this book; they are then no longer offering psychodynamic approach and is best to use a supportive approach.

In contrast, if the therapist is unsure if the patient would be able to use something more exploratory, they can review some of the criteria, based on Nina Coltart (1986), understanding of suitability for psychoanalysis:

- *Emotional Experience.* Can the patient engage with and make associations between their feelings?
- *Reflective Capacity.* Can they connect past experiences with present difficulties?
- *Reality Testing.* Can they clearly distinguish internal and external reality?
- *Curiosity and Insight.* Do they show a drive to understand their distress?

During the assessment, the therapist needs to balance the factors above with the reason for consultation, whether the patient is seeking to explore underlying issues or simply looking for support, also the number of session and length of treatment that can be provided. In many cases, there may not be a clear-cut answer, and the therapist can offer an open conversation with the patient about the different options available. Without becoming overly technical, the therapist can share what each approach might entail, allowing the patient to make an informed decision about the direction of their therapy.

External Support (Multidisciplinary Team)

External support refers to two key aspects: ensuring that sufficient resources are available to work safely with the patient, and determining whether the setting is appropriate for both the patient and the therapist. This includes collaboration with other agencies or specialists within the same team, and in private practice, having prior experience and established connections with relevant specialists in the area.

During the assessment process, therapists must gather all necessary information from the patient and evaluate their needs in relation to other agencies involved in their care. This ensures that the patient's needs are well-understood that an appropriate therapeutic approach is chosen and that the correct professionals are ready to intervene if necessary. Beginning supportive therapy without proper preparation and coordination with external agencies can lead to poor outcomes if the patient deteriorates and the therapist is unprepared to handle a complex situation.

It is crucial for therapists to feel confident and not out of their depth. If a therapist finds the circumstances too complex, this will likely affect the treatment, and the patient may sense this unease. Therefore, assessing the support available from other agencies and ensuring it is sufficient for safe practice is essential.

Examples:

- *Substance Misuse.* Therapists should have connections with rehabilitation centres, methadone clinics, and detox programmes. If a therapist lacks knowledge about detox processes or referral pathways, it may be best not to take the case. A multi-agency approach should be established from the outset.
- *Mood Disorders.* In cases of major depression or mania, it is crucial to have access to a skilled psychiatrist and a team of psychiatric nurses who can provide community-based interventions. For example, a psychiatrist may need to ensure safe sectioning for patients who experience manic and are currently sleeping in the streets.

If a patient discloses a diagnosis of bipolar disorder during the assessment, the therapist must explore their history and ensure that appropriate support is in place in case of relapse. In my experience supervising trainees in placement, I have seen how, in charities facing external pressures, therapy often begins without sufficient preparation, leading to a scramble for support when the patient deteriorates. In contrast, NHS settings are typically better prepared for early intervention by referring from the beginning to an established mental health team that can provide support. In the UK, if a patient is already known to mental health services, support can be provided quickly. However, if they are not, it can take months just to receive an assessment. This preparation should be in place from the beginning. Having said this, the situation in the NHS keeps changing, and patients who are unwell are constantly being discharged from appropriate teams, due to waiting list and service demands. In this circumstance, knowing the teams and how to navigate their systems becomes even more important. What the therapist needs to avoid is a patient in a crisis, which then requires a different team and a therapist who then loses hope. Or alternatively, a patient who attends Accident and Emergency (A&E) and receives inappropriate interventions which do not deliver the support required.

In private practice, I address this issue by making it part of my therapeutic agreement that, when needed, the patient must see a psychiatrist of my choosing. This ensures that, in the event of a relapse, I know who to contact and what to expect.

By integrating these assessments into clinical practice, therapists can tailor interventions and define their role within a multidisciplinary team to mitigate suicide risk, prevent harm to the patient and others, and promote overall well-being effectively within a supportive framework.

It is also essential to ensure that the setting is appropriate for the patient. Whether working in an office inside supportive accommodation, a mental health unit, a prison, or private practice, each environment presents unique challenges that must be considered to ensure the safety of both patient and therapist. For example, I previously worked in a probation unit (not in a therapeutic role) where each room had an alarm button and CCTV, and a police officer was always stationed at reception, where they could see the CCTV. Such settings can help therapists feel secure enough to engage in the work and fully understand all aspects of their patient, even the most perverse or aggressive, when this is a complex forensic case.

Therapist Competency

Therapists must ensure they have the necessary competencies and adequate support to handle complex cases. They need to be prepared for worst-case scenarios based on a patient's mental health history that indicates a clear need for expertise. A safe holding environment is one where the therapist can provide support beyond simply referring the patient back to their GP in a crisis. If a therapist feels uneasy about starting treatment, they should reflect on the reasons for this and consider an extended assessment period to ensure they are fully prepared for the case. If the therapist is out of their comfort zone, they will struggle to offer support, particularly if they feel anxious or unsettled by the patient's presentation.

Practitioners must be prepared for the unique challenges that come with each presentation. This includes being aware of their own limitations, having a solid understanding of the patient's condition, and ensuring appropriate support systems are in place. By doing so, therapists can create a truly safe and supportive environment that fosters a sense of safety in the professionalism and knowledge of the therapist.

An example of why previous knowledge on specific areas is important can be seen when working with patients recovering from heroin addiction. A standard assessment question should always include inquiries about blood or urine samples. Failing to ask about this during the initial assessment would be seen as poor practice.

The reason for this is simple: for patients using methadone clinics, doctors often refuse to continue prescribing methadone unless they have an up-to-date blood sample in some cases or urine samples when they like to monitor drug intake. If a patient is also using heroin alongside methadone, their test results will reveal this, and many doctors, especially those who are less experienced, will immediately stop the methadone prescription. A more experienced doctor might explore alternative approaches, but this is not always the case.

The key issue here is that if a patient is suddenly cut off from methadone, they are highly likely to disengage from treatment altogether. Methadone is a substitute for heroin and patients will struggle without it. This was a consistent pattern in my work with heroin-dependent patients, once methadone became unavailable, their sense of trust and safety was severely disrupted, making it incredibly difficult to reconnect with the service later.

Furthermore, patients often feel unsafe reducing or stopping heroin use if they believe methadone will not be reliably available. This highlights the critical role of methadone consistency within an integrated and well-coordinated support system. A therapist working in this context must understand these dynamics and collaborate closely with medical teams to ensure that patients receive continuous and structured care, forming a crucial part of a truly supportive environment. At the same time there are complications for patients who had used heroin that the therapist needs to know. For example, if they need pain medication, this may become problematic because it is often the case that even high doses of prescribed painkillers do nothing for them, as their body is already tolerant to heroin. Something as trivial as a dentist appointment can become a reason for relapse. For example, I worked with a man who didn't take any painkillers after breaking his arm. The doctor, who knew his problems with addiction, suggested only paracetamol, but the patient knew this would do nothing for him and didn't want anything stronger as he feared relapse.

The therapist also needs to have a realistic understanding of what can be expected from a patient. In substance-misuse cases, for instance, simply showing up for therapy, even if late, can be considered a significant achievement. A less experienced therapist might feel the need to push for more, not recognizing that even minimal participation can be a meaningful step in the right direction.

This mismatch in expectations can negatively impact treatment. Therapists may feel disappointed in their work (when, in reality, they are providing excellent care) and start pushing the patient towards something they can't do, simply because they imposed inappropriate expectations. This often comes from a limited understanding of specific mental health conditions and the reality that, for example, some mood disorders are chronic and require long-term management rather than fundamental transformation.

Evaluating a therapist's competency is even more crucial when working with complex cases that represent a high risk. This involves considering their experience with specific diagnoses and their ability to function within a multidisciplinary framework.

As examples:

1. *Mood Disorders.* A therapist who is also a psychiatric nurse will approach supportive therapy with a patient suffering from a mood disorder with a clear awareness of potential challenges. They will understand the role of a multidisciplinary team in managing these difficulties, ensuring they are equipped to intervene effectively when needed.
2. *Personality Disorders.* A therapist with experience working in an NHS personality disorder unit will be far better prepared to manage the complexities of a patient with borderline personality disorder who self-harms. The same applies to forensic patients or those who suffered from PTSD. Experience in specialized placements, such as the Portman Clinic for forensic patients or the Tavistock Trauma Unit for trauma patients, along with relevant training, is far more valuable than a brief theoretical understanding of these conditions or seniority on their associations and institutions.
3. *Substance Misuse.* Many approaches to substance misuse tend to be overly directive, making it challenging to balance support with addressing acting-out and setting boundaries. Therapists must be familiar with external agencies that provide detox, methadone clinics and rehab services, as we have seen, but also should have a clinical experience of working with relapse and when and how it is pertinent to intervene.

In summary, it is crucial for the therapist to know their limits. If a therapist or patient does not feel safe, it is a horrible place to be for both. It is hard to care for a patient you feel you can't help and hard for the patient to open up to someone that will not be able to support them when they are most needed, who manifests nervousness and distress.

There are many patients I choose not to take on; not because I believe supportive interventions would be unsuitable, but because I am not the right therapist for them due to my training, experience, and limitations. Knowing when to accept a patient and when to decline, demonstrates professionalism and experience.

I emphasize this because it is an important lesson, one that took me years to learn. More experienced practitioners do not take on complex cases or put themselves in difficult situations unless all the necessary requirements are in place. It is often the less experienced clinician, eager to prove themselves, who takes on unsuitable cases, sometimes with harmful consequences.

The same pattern can be seen in charitable organizations which, out of a genuine desire to help, often find themselves handling cases that an NHS therapeutic Trust would never take, and they would refer to a specialist. When this constantly happens, one can see many patients that have a long history of therapeutic interventions, but none of them lasting, and probably in retrospect, more harmful than useful.

Competency does not mean taking on a difficult case and excelling; it means knowing when to take a case, when to decline, and when to wait until the right conditions are in place. True knowledge is not just about treating patients, it is about having the experience to articulate what is required to start therapeutic work and why.

Long Assessment

As mentioned before, I recommend conducting two assessment sessions, which is the standard practice in psychoanalysis. For example, when I was conducting assessments for the BPA (British Psychoanalytic Association), this was our process. However, there are times when we are uncertain or confused about a case. Instead of rushing into offering a decision, there is an informal approach known as a *long assessment*, which simply means extending the assessment period with additional sessions until the therapist gains a clearer sense of whether therapy will be beneficial.

When working with an EAP (Employee Assistance Program), we sometimes offered up to six sessions of extended assessment. This was mainly because the number of sessions available for treatment was limited, and we were unsure whether we could offer further support. In these cases, extending the assessment provided a practical approach that allowed for a more thoughtful decision, rather than a rushed one.

References

American Psychological Association. (2016, November 1). *Experts' ability to predict suicidal behaviors no better than chance.* https://www.apa.org/news/press/releases/2016/11/suicidal-behaviors

Bateman, A. W. (1998). Thick- and Thin-Skinned Organisations and Enactment in Borderline and Narcissistic Disorders. *The International Journal of Psycho-Analysis, 79*, 13–25.

Britton, R. (2003). *Sex, Death, and the Superego: Experiences in Psychoanalysis.* Karnac Books.

Britton, R. (2005). Re-enactment as an Unwitting Professional Act. In P. Perelberg (Ed.), *The Oedipus Complex Today* (pp. 98–112). Karnac Books.

Brüdern, J., Stähli, A., Gysin-Maillart, A., Michel, K., Reisch, T., & Jobes, D. (2018). Reasons for Living and Dying in Suicide Attempters: A Two-Year Prospective Study. *BMC Psychiatry, 18*, 234. https://doi.org/10.1186/s12888-018-1814-8

Ciarrochi, J., & Mayer, J. D. (Eds.). (2007). *Applying Emotional Intelligence: A Practitioner's Guide*. Psychology Press.

Coltart, N. E. (1986). Diagnosis and Assessment of Suitability for Psychoanalytic Psychotherapy. *Contemporary Psychoanalysis, 22*, 560–569.

Diamond, D., Yeomans, F. E., Stern, B. L., & Kernberg, O. F. (2021). *Treating Pathological Narcissism with Transference-Focused Psychotherapy.* Guilford Publications.

Hinshelwood, R. D. (1991). Psychodynamic Formulation in Assessment for Psychotherapy. *British Journal of Psychotherapy, 8*, 166–174.

Kernberg, O. F. (1984a). *Severe Personality Disorders: Psychotherapeutic Strategies.* Yale University Press.

Kernberg, O. F. (1984b). The structural interview. In *Severe Personality Disorders* (pp. 27–51). Yale University Press.

Kernberg, O. F. (2019a). *Psychoanalytic Education at the Crossroads: A Report to the American Psychoanalytic Association*. Routledge.

Kernberg, O. F. (2019b). Psychotic Personality Structure. *Psychodynamic Psychiatry, 47*, 353–372.

Leichsenring, F., & Rabung, S. (2011). Long-Term Psychodynamic Psychotherapy in Complex Mental Disorders: Update of a Meta-Analysis. *British Journal of Psychiatry, 199*(1), 15–22. https://doi.org/10.1192/bjp.bp.110.082776

Lemma, A. (2009). Being Seen or Being Watched? A Psychoanalytic Perspective on Body Dysmorphia. *International Journal of Psychoanalysis, 90*, 753–771.

Luborsky, L. (1984). *Principles of Psychoanalytic Psychotherapy: A Manual for Supportive-Expressive Treatment*. Basic Books.

Luborsky, L., Barber, J. P., & Crits-Christoph, P. (1990). *Theory and Practice of Supportive-Expressive Psychodynamic Therapy.* Basic Books.

Mackinnon, R. A., Michels, R., & Buckley, P. (2016). *The Psychiatric Interview in Clinical Practice*. American Psychiatric Association Publishing.
Malan, D. H. (1976). *The Frontier of Brief Psychotherapy: An Example of the Convergence of Research and Clinical Practice*. Plenum Press.
Milton, J. (1997). Why Assess? Psychoanalytical Assessment in the NHS. *Psychoanalytic Psychotherapy, 11*, 47–58.
Qin, P., Agerbo, E., & Mortensen, P. B. (2002). Suicide Risk in Relation to Family History of Completed Suicide and Psychiatric Disorders: A Nested Case-Control Study Based on Longitudinal Registers. *The Lancet, 360*(9340), 1126–1130. https://doi.org/10.1016/S0140-6736(02)11197-4
Rosenfeld, H. (1987). *Impasse and Interpretation*. Routledge.
Shedler, J. (2010). The Efficacy of Psychodynamic Psychotherapy. *American Psychologist, 65*(2), 98–109.
The Erikson Institute of the Austen Riggs Center. (2018). Integrative Psychodynamic Model for Understanding and Assessing the Suicidal Patient. *Psychoanalytic Psychology, 35*(4), 424–432.

CHAPTER 4

Introduction to the Fundamentals of Supportive Therapy

Introduction to the Fundamentals of Supportive Therapy

When I supervise therapists and students, I prioritize three key aspects that help me create a frame of mind I can use to understand their work. First, is the setting; second is the therapeutic alliance; and third is the supportive work, or "working through" in the case of psychodynamic psychotherapy. While these elements are interconnected and sometimes interchangeable, they follow a necessary sequence. A supportive process cannot exist without a strong therapeutic alliance, and a therapeutic alliance cannot develop without a solid setting.

For example, a problematic contemporary practice is allowing patients to book sessions through an online platform, choosing an hour at the patients' convenience. This model is highly unreliable and fosters a consumer mentality rather than a therapeutic one. It is often marketed under the false premise of "empowering the patient," but in reality, it establishes an uncommitted, transactional relationship that undermines the therapeutic process.

A patient of mine previously attended therapy with a practitioner who used this system. After a session in which he disclosed deeply personal material, he attempted to book another appointment, only to find no availability the following week. He had no clear sense of when his therapist

R. S. Escandon, *Contemporary Developments in Supportive Therapy*, Palgrave Texts in Counselling and Psychotherapy, https://doi.org/10.1007/978-3-031-96059-8_4

would be accessible, making it impossible to establish a reliable, consistent process, a fundamental requirement for meaningful therapeutic work. Furthermore, the reason why he disclosed something personal is that although he was not feeling comfortable, he wanted to give therapy a proper go. He risked opening up but was then left alone.

Once a solid setting is established, the next crucial step is building a strong therapeutic alliance, as this is essential for any supportive intervention to be effective. Without this foundation, patients may struggle to engage or commit to the process. True supportive work can only occur when the patient trusts in both the therapist's consistent presence and the reliability of the process itself. Let's review in detail this characteristic.

The Setting

The setting can be understood as a "pact," an agreement between the patient and the therapist that outlines the conditions under which the therapeutic work will take place (Sparer, 2024). This is usually discussed after the assessment and formalized in a contract that both the therapist and patient agree to (as we will see in the following section).

The role of the setting differs between supportive therapy and psychoanalytic approaches. In psychoanalytic treatment, the setting serves as a stable framework that contains the patient's experience while facilitating the emergence of transference and unconscious phantasies (Lemma, 2016). In contrast, supportive interventions take a different approach; rather than encouraging deep transference exploration, the focus is on creating a sense of comfort and security, ensuring the patient feels safe enough to engage without becoming overwhelmed.

The setting consists of two main components: the material framework and the analytic stance. The material framework refers to the external, contractual, and structural elements that define the analytic encounter. These are the fixed, explicit rules such as session frequency, duration, location, payment policies, and holiday interruptions, as well as the therapist's ability to uphold the agreement. They create a stable and predictable environment necessary for the therapeutic work to take place. The analytic stance involves the therapist's emotional availability, neutrality, abstinence, and attentiveness, as well as their overall approach, which remains consistent session after session.

The analytic stance reflects the therapist's disciplined restraint in not responding impulsively or habitually. Unlike typical social interactions, the therapy setting is carefully structured to create a space conducive to healing. It involves the therapist's internal position, which shapes both their approach and the relationship with the patient, all grounded in the purpose of the psychotherapeutic encounter (Temperley, 1984).

By holding back their own emotions, the therapist allows the therapeutic space to be shaped by the patient's experience. For example, imagine discussing a politically charged topic with a close friend. In this informal setting, you might express yourself passionately, laugh, or even make an impulsive inappropriate comment. This kind of spontaneous exchange is common in social interactions, but the boundaries between each person's emotions can blur. In therapy, however, when a patient brings up a controversial topic, the therapist doesn't offer their opinion. Instead, they seek to understand the symbolic meaning behind the topic, whether the patient is testing boundaries, seeking a reaction, or connecting the issue to something within the therapeutic relationship.

The knowledge that someone is consistently present at a fixed time each week, ready to listen, provides reassurance and gradually fosters an emotional bond. Predictability is a crucial aspect of the setting, especially for patients whose early experiences were shaped by unreliable or inconsistent caregivers (Holmes, 2016). Winnicott (1955) highlighted that a stable therapeutic environment nurtures trust, much like early caregiving experiences characterized by consistency. The therapist's reliability serves as a symbolic reparation for these early relational wounds, creating a dependable framework for therapeutic work. For instance, a patient raised by a volatile parent may find it difficult to express vulnerability, fearing unpredictable reactions. A steady and predictable therapist can help ease these anxieties, allowing the patient to engage more fully in the process.

Winnicott (1965) emphasized that a facilitating environment depends on the therapist's capacity to be emotionally in tune with the patient, offering a non-judgemental space that supports autonomy and emotional openness. A key distinction must be made between responsiveness and reactivity: the former involves a thoughtful, attuned engagement with the patient's emotional world, while the latter can introduce unhelpful disruptions. Even small gestures, such as acknowledging a patient's distress, can serve as meaningful signs, reinforcing a sense of being heard and understood.

The therapist must maintain emotional containment, regardless of their personal circumstances. A fundamental aspect of the analytic stance is ensuring that sessions remain centred on the patient, which can be challenging if the therapist is preoccupied with their own difficulties. This is particularly difficult during times of personal emotional strain for the therapist.

There are two key considerations in managing this. First, in situations such as bereavement, the therapist taking time off work may be the most responsible and ethical choice. Second, therapists need to cultivate a sense of ease in their work environment. For me, something as simple as having a good coffee before sessions and ensuring I have a comfortable chair in a quiet, uninterrupted space makes a significant difference. Each therapist will find their own ways to prepare; some may go to the gym or practice yoga beforehand. Ultimately, being fully present for the patient requires self-awareness and an ability to sustain consistency. The key is to avoid a situation where the therapist becomes genuinely fragile, shifting the dynamic so that the patient feels the need to care for them.

Changes to the setting, such as adjusting session times, transitioning to online formats, or altering the consultant's office, can provoke diverse responses from patients, particularly those with neurotic tendencies. Some may remain unaware, while others could experience significant anxiety, perceiving these changes as symbolic of past relational issues where change is synonymous with something negative. Even the therapist's physical presence, the way they sit, breathe, move within the space, speak, and even dress, forms an integral part of the sensory experience of the setting. These elements contribute to the containment offered by the therapist, a concept Lemma (2016) refers to as the "embodied setting." It is crucial to minimize changes in a supportive environment whenever possible. Changes can become problematic in supportive work because the goal is not to explore the anxiety surrounding these changes or the transference, but rather to create a space that is as safe as possible, with minimal anxiety.

The setting also serves as an ongoing extension of the therapeutic agreement. The therapist must maintain clear boundaries throughout the treatment, especially with challenging patients who might test these boundaries. For example, boundaries around behaviour, such as prohibiting physical contact or destructive actions, are essential for maintaining a safe environment (Kernberg, 2003). If these boundaries aren't upheld, the therapeutic process could be compromised. For instance, in substance misuse treatment, a standard rule is that sessions cannot occur if the patient is intoxicated. While this boundary is frequently tested, it is essential to maintain it to safeguard the integrity of the process and prevent the complications that may arise from allowing such behaviour.

When therapy is conducted within a multidisciplinary framework, such as in NHS settings, the professionalism of administrative staff and the multidisciplinary team also contributes to the therapeutic setting. Their role, though often behind the scenes, is essential to creating a stable and supportive environment for the patient. As Taylor (2015) emphasized, a patient's openness depends on a reliable environment, this includes the wider staff that will work with the patient.

Finally, a consistent setting is one that can address clinical dilemmas directly, ensuring they are not avoided but carefully worked through.

The following anecdote illustrates how the setting, even in seemingly trivial matters, can influence the therapeutic process. It involves a patient who had been attending therapy for several months and was making good progress. During one of the sessions, she came with wet red paint on her trousers and when she left the couch was soiled with the paint and damaged.

Rather than simply ignoring the damage or reacting dismissively, the therapist helped the patient take responsibility in a constructive way, resulting in the patient paying for it to be cleaned. It was crucial not to disregard what the patient had done, as this could feel highly persecutory, especially for a patient struggling with reparation; someone whose personal history has been marked by punishment without the opportunity to amend relationships. In supportive therapy, the solution was to provide the patient with a way out, one that is the less anxiety provoking.

Contract or Therapeutic Agreement

Establishing a therapeutic contract or agreement should occur immediately after the assessment phase and before the therapeutic process begins. This agreement is essential to all forms of psychotherapy, not just supportive therapy, as it lays the foundation for the mutual understanding between the patient and therapist, outlining the nature of the setting (Werman, 1984). The contract should clearly define key elements such as therapy expectations, session times, and confidentiality while maintaining a structured yet flexible approach to accommodate the patient's evolving needs.

Clear communication regarding roles and expectations is a fundamental principle in various therapeutic approaches and crucial for a successful process (Werman, 1984; Pinsker, 1997; Hass & Ardell, 2020). These principles ensure the therapeutic process remains transparent, mutually agreed upon, and focused on improving the patient's well-being by providing a predictable and consistent framework.

It's crucial to eliminate any ambiguity regarding payment schedules, cancellation policies, holiday arrangements, and the possibility of working online. Therapists must avoid improvisation or vague commitments. For instance, if a therapist adjusts their fees annually, this should be communicated at the outset, rather than midway through the therapy process.

It's important to distinguish between the flexibility inherent in supportive therapy and inconsistency or lack of clarity. At no point should the patient be uncertain about the time, date, and location of future sessions; there should be no "on the go" scheduling. Flexibility can include rescheduling one or two sessions, adding an extra session when the patient is in distress, or taking a scheduled phone call outside of session times if the patient is distressed. However, flexibility should always be considered within the framework of the agreed-upon setting, with consideration for the reason behind the adjustment. For example, it may be more beneficial for the patient to agree to a second session during the week or to include a home treatment team as part of the setting, rather than repeatedly having phone calls outside the agreed time.

In contemporary practice, clear communication about online sessions from the start is essential. When a patient is away or unwell, transitioning to online sessions has become common practice. Whether the therapist offers a blended (face to face and online) approach or not should be clarified when agreeing on the setting. Additionally, the parameters for online sessions must be clearly communicated. For instance, sessions held in public spaces like coffee shops or parks should not be considered acceptable. If the session is to be held at home, the patient must ensure privacy and comfort, ensuring no one else can overhear the conversation.

Henry Pinsker (1997) emphasizes the importance of the patient consenting to be an active participant in the therapeutic process. He stresses the necessity of collaboration to align both parties towards a shared therapeutic process. This is why the patient should be given the opportunity to provide input and request changes when the setting is being agreed upon. The therapeutic agreement should not be imposed on the patient. For example, if a patient frequently travels for work and the therapist does not offer blended sessions, the patient may need to find a different therapist.

In supportive therapy, it's important for the patient to understand that the goal is not to immediately solve problems or develop specific strategies. Rather, the space provided is flexible, and it is up to the patient to explore how they wish to use it.

I don't necessarily define the role of supportive therapy explicitly when offering the contract, but I ensure this has been explored beforehand; usually during the assessment when I ask about the patient's expectations. If there is uncertainty, before presenting the contract, I might say, *"I can offer you a supportive space that will be consistently available for you to talk about what you are going through."* If a patient asks about specific strategies or expects something beyond what supportive therapy offers, I clarify this and may suggest Cognitive Behavioural Therapy (CBT) as an alternative. Similarly, if a patient assumes that therapy will eliminate a symptom, I address this directly, making it clear that this is not our goal. Revisiting expectations identified during the assessment phase is also standard practice to ensure a mutual understanding (Caligor et al., 2018).

Talking about what supportive therapy will entail, at the point of establishing the contract, helps assess whether the therapy model fits the patient's needs. Many patients feel relieved knowing they will have a consistent, open space rather than a short-term intervention focused only on symptoms. However, if a patient struggles to see how this will help them, it's a sign that a deeper conversation about their expectations and needs is necessary.

Setting clear expectations in therapy is essential, yet the outcome is never entirely predictable. Ogden (2016) describes psychoanalytic work as inherently unfinished, while Freud (1937) saw termination as a practical choice rather than a sign that all conflicts had been resolved. In supportive therapy, endings are even more fluid, guided by when a patient no longer feels the need for support, something highly personal and difficult to define in advance.

For example, a patient with eczema or asthma might experience an improvement in their physical symptoms through therapy, perhaps due to reduced anxiety or increased awareness of emotional triggers. However, it would be inappropriate to suggest that therapy can cure their condition. Instead, we can explain that while therapy provides a supportive space that may indirectly enhance well-being, it does not aim to treat physical symptoms.

Therapeutic Alliance

The concept of the therapeutic alliance gained prominence in the 1950s and 1960s through authors like Zetzel (1956) and Greenson (1965), who emphasized collaboration between therapist and patient. This marked a shift from an exclusive focus on interpretation and transference towards a more relational approach, where the alliance itself was seen as crucial to therapeutic progress.

However, authors such as Goldberger (2008) and Brenner (1979) argued that it is not enough to acknowledge the presence of an alliance; one must understand why a patient engages in analytic work and tolerates the intimacy of the therapeutic relationship. For me, this means that whether one interprets or not, the essential factor is the therapist's capacity to hold a psychoanalytic way of thinking within the relationship. What patients come to value is not the therapist's likability, but their ability to think and relate in this way. That said, if the patient happens to like you, the work can feel easier for both.

Greenson (1965) described the therapeutic alliance as the therapist's consistent and unwavering pursuit of insight in response to all aspects of the patient's material and behaviour. He cautioned against confrontation, which could provoke defensiveness, and instead advocated for gentler ways of engaging the patient. This approach fosters cooperation by establishing a partnership rather than a hierarchical relationship in which the analyst is the sole authority. Similarly, Novalis et al. (1993) emphasized the role of empathy in strengthening the alliance, as it helps patients feel understood and valued on a deeper emotional level.

A strong therapeutic relationship is widely recognized as a key predictor of positive outcomes and is particularly vital in supportive psychotherapy, especially for patients with attachment difficulties or personality disorders (Carsky, 2013). These patients may struggle with fears of abandonment, feelings of inadequacy, or rage triggered by their dependency on the therapist. Paradoxically, the very efforts to provide a stable and supportive setting can provoke anxiety, leading the patient to react against it.

I often encountered this when working with homelessness; patients who were offered stable housing, food security, and financial support would sometimes sabotage these opportunities. Living without having their basic needs met was, paradoxically, easier than receiving help while fearing its eventual loss. I see a similar dynamic in therapy: as patients begin to feel heard and emotionally held, they may also experience a growing hunger for therapy, only to then fear their own dependency and doubt whether the therapist can truly be reliable. When this happens, the patient needs to believe they are "in good hands."

When a patient is particularly difficult or unpleasant, authors like Lester Luborsky (1984) recommend identifying aspects of the patient to appreciate. While this might initially feel forced, the idea is to find something genuinely likeable within the patient's personality. Similarly, Winnicott (1949) suggests that recognizing the underlying reasons for a patient's anger or frustration can shift the therapist's perspective, fostering a more empathetic stance.

Ultimately, genuinely caring for the patient is the ideal foundation for therapeutic work, but this is not always possible. In such cases, ongoing reflection on countertransference can offer valuable insight into the patient's internal world. In my experience, this process also fosters the therapist's curiosity, which in turn makes the patient feel valued.

Once the therapist has secured a therapeutic alliance, supportive interventions can be offered. What I mean by this is that there is now a therapeutic couple working towards the same goal. However, if the patient is uncertain or if there are consistent issues with the setting, these elements should be addressed first.

In a strong therapeutic alliance, the patient may express anger or be harsh; a good alliance is not necessarily one where there is always warmth or harmony. Instead, a solid therapeutic relationship is one in which the patient can bring anything, including anger or accusations, while trusting that these feelings will be managed within the therapeutic couple and that the relationship will survive. For example, patients with borderline personality disorder often threaten to leave treatment. Rather than being solely a sign of rupture, this can indicate a strong alliance, as the patient feels safe enough to repeatedly bring conflict into the space, knowing that the relationship can withstand it. More often than not, they are threatening the therapist because of this familiarity, which is part of their dynamic when they get close to others.

In supportive therapy, the debate between prioritizing a strong therapeutic alliance and maintaining a strict analytic stance should be understood in terms of support, rather than exploration. The classical analytic approach, characterized by rigid abstinence and neutrality, is designed to foster regression and allow the patient to unconsciously develop a fantasy of the therapist, projecting their ways of relating, including anxieties, feelings of love, hate, and desire, with the purpose of exploration. However, as we know, exploration is not the focus of supportive therapy. Furthermore, many analysts argue that patients may not fully grasp the unique nature of the analytic setting, where withholding information or maintaining neutrality is not mistreatment but a technical necessity (Abend, 1999).

For this reason, there is no need for the therapist to be silent, abstinent, or strictly neutral. The challenge is to maintain the therapeutic role without unnecessary creating a tense atmosphere, that will work against the supportive attitude. What does this look like in practice?

The therapist can offer reassurance at times, avoid unnecessary negative transference, clarify any misunderstanding, answer direct questions, and cultivate a more friendly and natural relationship, one that prevents the patient from projecting disinterest or rejection onto the therapist. As Adler (1999) suggests, early interventions should aim to reduce ambiguity to prevent fragmentation, offering direct clarifications (e.g. naming misunderstandings) and explicit safety measures (such as crisis plans) to create a stabilizing holding environment. Countertransference, often intensified by projective identifications (feelings of worthlessness or helplessness), requires vigilant containment and interpretation to avoid conflating the therapist's needs with the patient's progress.

The therapist needs to face their own discomfort with intense emotions like hopelessness or grief, without abandoning the supportive approach in favour of a more problem-solving attitude. While this shift may seem helpful, it can actually reflect the therapist's difficulty in tolerating the patient's pain and the emotional weight of the session. This is not the type of flexibility that is recommended. The real therapeutic work lies in being with the patient in their darkest moments, tolerating their pain without attempting to push it away. Though this may not seem impressive on the surface, it is one of the most profoundly healing aspects of supportive therapy. As we will explore below, there are other forms of flexibility, such as disclosing, reassuring, and responding to the patient's narrative, that are more permissible in supportive therapy, as they help avoid negative transference.

Finally, it is important to recognize that the therapeutic alliance is not something established at the outset and then simply maintained. When working with borderline and narcissistic patients, the alliance should be seen as an ongoing process throughout treatment rather than a foundational starting point. These patients, often shaped by histories of neglect, abandonment, or critical caregivers, may lack the early relational experiences necessary to sustain collaborative trust. As a result, maintaining a positive alliance is an ongoing process that the therapist must work through at every stage of treatment (Adler, 1999)

Exploratory Versus Support

The primary aim of supportive therapy is not exploration, though exploration remains an important aspect of any therapeutic process. The focus is on creating a supportive setting and fostering a strong therapeutic alliance that helps the patient feel better and provides an emotional outlet for their conflicts. A common misconception is that this characteristic can be found in most therapeutic approaches.

If the goal of psychodynamic therapy is exploration, this should be explicitly reflected in the interventions, not just through more interpretations but also through the aim in which other interventions are used, which guide the narrative towards self-awareness, regression, or into a deeper exploration by challenging resistance.

When offering psychodynamic psychotherapy or psychoanalysis, although I may not always be interpreting, I still take on an analytic role with the aim of uncovering or exploring unconscious dynamics. This involves fostering regression with a stand-back attitude, where my interventions aim to help the patient think in relation to the emotions initiating in the transference. This process inevitably requires examining elements of the session the patient may be reluctant to explore or assimilate about themselves. It also involves exploring emotional pain in a way, which seeks to expand and uncover more, bringing memories and fantasies. This process is painful and anxiety-provoking.

Additionally, exploratory therapies should allow the negative transference to develop. For example, a patient who had been suffering verbal abuse from her husband asked him to leave the house, and he complied. The following week, the patient shared a slightly different version of her husband, one in which he was more aggressive and was clearly having a negative impact on their children. She hadn't told me this before, so I said, "You are showing me a different version of your husband." What I was thinking was that now that her husband was out of the house, she felt it was safe enough to confront the most difficult part of his behaviour in therapy. However, what she thought was that I didn't believe her or thought she was exaggerating.

She was a patient attending multiple sessions a week and had the resilience for psychodynamic therapy. I didn't correct her misconception, and she quickly turned me into a bad person. At this point, I think I was holding her own feelings of guilt, of being a bad person for kicking her husband out. In psychodynamic therapy, the therapeutic alliance can tolerate this. However, a more vulnerable patient might leave the therapy feeling accused or misunderstood. In psychodynamic therapy, once the negative transference has developed, we can see how she projected onto me her own feelings about herself. This is exploration. In supportive therapy, however, this level of exploration cannot be tolerated by the patient, so they are actively avoided.

In contrast, when I was managing a service for women experiencing homelessness and domestic abuse, we often encountered patients who would only engage on their own terms and struggled with attendance. For many, this meant adhering to a strict narrative in which their ex-partner was solely an abuser and they were entirely a victim; any deviation was perceived as victim-blaming. In such cases, the therapeutic relationship could not withstand negative transference, often leading to disengagement. Implementing exploratory interventions instead of a supportive approach would have been a mistake.

The therapist's mindset is crucial, regardless of the intervention or the handling of negative transference. I have often seen students and supervisees make mistakes when supportive therapy is required, and their mindset is of exploration. If a therapist approaches treatment with the belief that success depends on discovery, uncovering unconscious material, or expanding awareness, they inevitably steer the therapeutic narrative in that direction. In moments of emotional pain, the therapist might fail to offer empathy, opting instead for curiosity, which is not well received by the patient.

This is highly problematic because, if the assessment has been conducted properly, the patient in supportive therapy will not benefit from a therapist who persistently tries to explore. It is even more concerning when therapists use interpretation to "uncover" something or challenge resistance. In supportive therapy, patients require assistance in strengthening or rebuilding their defences, not in dismantling them.

The idea that discussions of conflict and exploration can be distressing is well established, as demonstrated in the work of Van der Kolk (2015), Shapiro et al. (2007), and in EMDR practices. Patients often leave the sessions feeling worse and interrupt the treatment. Therefore, supportive therapy requires a different mindset, one that prioritizes the patient feeling heard, understood, and stabilized. A key distinction from traditional psychodynamic therapy is that, in supportive interventions, if a patient feels better at the end of a session, the therapist has done a good job. In contrast, psychodynamic therapy often involves engaging with emotional pain as an integral part of the process, and patients may leave sessions in distress, with much to think about during the time between sessions.

Exploration raises defences and creates distress; this is something all psychoanalytic therapists encounter regularly. Supportive therapy requires more than simply understanding when exploration may not be the right approach at a given moment; it requires a mindset or ongoing attitude that differs from exploration. The emphasis should be on containing the patient's emotional experience while trying to understand their need for using primitive defences.

That said, different therapists may mean different things when they refer to exploration. Therapy, at its core, is an exploratory journey into the patient's unconscious dynamics just by fostering a relationship (Carrère, 2008). Even in supportive work, some level of exploration inevitably takes place. The therapeutic journey, even when not explicitly focused on exploration, still allows for significant emotional learning, insights about themself that the patient may not have had before. For instance, if therapy is conducted effectively with a challenging patient, they may come to understand, perhaps for the first time, what it feels like to allow someone to care for them. The experience of being understood and contained in therapy carries profound significance, often more than what is explicitly said (Allison & Fonagy, 2016). This raises an important question: what do we mean by exploration?

Bion (1965) observed that patients' emotional experiences can be transformed through their interaction with the therapist and the therapeutic environment. If we define exploration and this kind of transformation, as the creation of a safe space that enables change, then supportive therapy undoubtedly facilitates this process. However, if exploration is primarily understood as the pursuit of insight, the uncovering of unconscious material, the working through of memories and resistance, or the use of interpretation for the exploration of free association, as is often the case in psychodynamic and analytic therapy, then such an approach would not be considering supportive therapy and could even be iatrogenic.

Function of Supportive Therapy

To understand why supportive therapy is effective, the therapist must appreciate the transformative function of listening. Here is an anecdote that might help to express this idea:

> A few years ago, I was on the London Underground when the train abruptly stopped at a station, and the doors didn't open. A distressed driver apologized, assuring passengers that we would be able to leave shortly. We moved to a different carriage and exited. After exiting, we were informed that a person had jumped onto the tracks and was in critical condition under our carriage.

Once outside the underground station, I walked to a small convenience store. As I paid for a bottle of water, I told the cashier what had just happened. He barely reacted as he was likely accustomed to the endless stream of people passing through in a city as busy as London.

I left feeling uneasy as if I had shared too much or made a mistake. I wasn't seeking reassurance, advice, or any form of intervention. I simply needed someone to listen to what I had just gone through. The act of listening, without any response or interpretation, can be incredibly powerful. It allows the internal conflict to be externalized, offering a form of catharsis. Sometimes this is necessary because the experience itself is too intense, like witnessing a death. At other times, it's because the person is unable to process their emotions fully in the moment. In these instances, listening is not just valuable but essential.

For reflection to take place, an individual must first regulate their emotions by repressing part of the affect. This allows for mindful engagement with their feelings rather than reacting impulsively through actions like shouting or fighting. Only then can processing beyond the mere evacuation of distress occur. A listening ear, then, becomes a receptacle, a container and emotional regulator for emotional expression rather than for words or content. In *The Ego and the Id* (1923), Freud describes a version of humanity that struggles to function under the weight of internal desires, moral constraints, and external reality. He expresses sympathy for the Ego, which must navigate these three cruel rulers. If the Ego, as we saw in the section on defence mechanisms, cannot manoeuvre around intense experiences to integrate or tolerate them, then the distress becomes too great, and defences are used. We cannot, therefore, expect the struggling Ego to become reflective, engage in meaningful processes of association, or be able to use complex interventions.

Bion (1962) described how experiences, when raw and unprocessed, can be too overwhelming to understand. The therapist acts as a container, being present to receive the patient's distress. In an ideal therapeutic setting, the therapist processes the experience and returns something more manageable for the patient. Transforming a negative experience into something that can be worked through is not always possible in therapy; this is why the patient often feels the need to repeatedly retell their story. The supportive therapist is doing a good job if they have become a constant recipient of such stories and emotions, even if the patient and therapist can't yet do much with them.

In my case, I didn't need an intellectual reflection on human fragility from the cashier. I didn't need tools to cope with existential anxiety or a philosophical discussion on my own mortality. In moments of emotional intensity, what people often seek is a simple, yet profound human response: an acknowledgement of their emotional experience. This kind of response as Hellerstein et al. (1994) and Pinsker (1997) emphasize fosters trust and containment in therapy.

Active listening is about recognizing and holding the patient's emotional reality, providing a stabilizing presence that validates their distress without needing to solve it. In this sense, listening itself becomes a supportive action, one that shapes the therapeutic relationship. It is not merely hearing what a patient says but engaging with their experience in a deeply immersive way.

Listening in psychotherapy is not passive; it is a dynamic and layered process, the cornerstone of therapeutic efficacy, allowing the therapist to navigate both the patient's conscious and unconscious worlds. Through deep emotional connection, listening facilitates emotional healing and supports the reconfiguration of psychic realities (Meissner, 2000).

Language in therapy is not a fixed vehicle for meaning but a shifting, dynamic process where words carry deeply personal and often unconscious connotations. Derrida and Lacan argue that meaning is never fully stable but evolves as words interact within a chain of signifiers (Meissner, 2000). In psychoanalysis, this means that language does not provide absolute truths but offers a space where meaning can be explored, reinterpreted, and emotionally processed. Ultimately, relief comes from the ability to re-experience emotional realities through language (Wilson, 2018). Talking, just talking: simply telling a story with someone listening can heal; a therapist with a technical agenda can stop that from happening.

A major mistake made by therapists who apply supportive interventions is underestimating the profound impact of being listened to. They often rush towards problem-solving, interpretation, or exploration, assuming that these will be more effective. However, for many patients, especially those who struggle to articulate emotional distress, these approaches may be inaccessible, or the setting may not be recurrent enough for them to engage meaningfully.

If the therapist cannot step into the patient's subjective world and convey a genuine understanding of their internal states, if they cannot connect to what is psychically significant to the patient, then the patient cannot experience the therapist as a self-object capable of supporting their development. In such cases, either a misalliance by means of collusion will develop, or the therapy will break down entirely (Meissner, 2000).

Bion (1962) was deeply interested in the pre-verbal and emotional dimensions of experience and was sceptical of language's ability to fully capture emotional reality. He believed that emotional experience is best understood in the moment rather than through verbal descriptions which inevitably introduce distortion (Meissner, 2000). In many ways, what the cashier failed to do was to be receptive to my emotions.

Misunderstandings are common because language is inherently unstable; there is always a gap between the words we use and the experience we try to convey. Lacan's theory of the signifier and signified highlights that words do not have fixed meanings; they shift depending on context, much like looking up a word in a dictionary only leads to more words. Meaning is actively constructed through interpretation, which is why misunderstandings occur so frequently. We assume that words have static meanings when they are fluid and context-dependent (Wilson, 2018).

At the heart of supportive therapy, the therapist's mindset should not focus on extracting fixed meaning from language but on understanding its cathartic potential; the comfort it can provide simply through its expression.

Gabriel Sapisochin (2019) has explored the meaning of language beyond its semantic value in the consulting room. A patient's words carry more than just explicit meaning; they serve as vehicles for emotional expression, and they also play a crucial role in shaping the relationship between patient and therapist.

This is particularly relevant for patients who struggle with thirdness. These individuals often find it difficult to engage in a mutual process of meaning-making. Instead of tolerating the shared space where communication unfolds between two minds, they feel compelled to impose their own meaning. This is why interpretations can be so challenging for them: they represent the thoughts of the other, an external perspective that can feel intrusive rather than containing.

In supportive therapy, while we listen to what is being said (the semantic value), we also notice how it is said and what function it serves in the therapeutic relationship. The therapist needs to be attuned not only to the semantic and unconscious meanings but, most importantly, to the emotional value of language. This means following the emotional trajectory the patient assigns to words within their narrative.

Role of the Therapist

The therapist's role in supportive therapy is fundamentally one of alignment (being in touch with the patient's emotional state) and containment (providing a steady, receptive space for the patient' emotional experience). The therapist prioritizes deep listening, allowing the patient's inner world to unfold at its own pace, finding relief in the emotional expression.

To work effectively with a patient; thinking, generating hypotheses, and allowing the therapeutic process to evolve, therapists must approach each session with a willingness to rediscover the patient. Wilfred Bion's (1970) concept of working *without memory or desire* emphasizes maintaining openness and avoiding rigid preconceived notions. It invites the therapist to engage with each session as a fresh experience, resisting the temptation to rely too heavily on past formulations. If the therapist arrives at a particular understanding of the patient's conflict in one session, they must still approach the next with curiosity, ready to reassess and refine their perspective. This mindset fosters receptivity to new insights and a continually evolving understanding of the patient's experience. It also influences the way the therapist listens to their patient and how the patient feels listen to. This provides a clear distinction between brief supportive work and other interventions that begin with a formulation, which serves as a roadmap for the therapeutic process.

Working without memory or desire does not mean therapists should dismiss memory or previous knowledge entirely, as that would be both impractical and counterproductive. Memory provides continuity, offering essential context for understanding the patient's developmental history and recurring patterns. In fact, forgetting significant aspects of a patient's experience can be unsettling for both therapist and patient alike. Thoughtful integration of past knowledge allows therapists to deepen their comprehension of the patient's evolving dynamics rather than become confined by past interpretations.

Similarly, a therapist's own desires or inclinations in guiding the therapy process can serve as valuable indicators of countertransference. At times, these wishes or impulses may offer crucial insight into the patient's unconscious dynamics (Escandón, 2023). By attuning to these emotional responses, therapists can better understand the affective undercurrents shaping the therapeutic relationship.

Given that psychic reality is in constant flux, internal reality undergoes continual changes with each reorganization of the ego, leading to a continuous reconstruction of internal reality (Perez, 1996). What may have been a significant unconscious influence in one session might shift in importance in the next. Thus, the focus should be on being open to these changes and rediscovering the patient in each session. This approach is akin to the work of André Green (2002), who built on Freud's concept of nachträglichkeit to explore how meaning is always tied to the moment in which it is reconstructed. For Green, time is subjective rather than linear, representing multiple moments that repeat themselves. Each session should be understood as a singular moment rather than part of a linear progression. This contrasts with goal-oriented therapeutic approaches that treat therapy as a linear process moving towards a specific goal.

The therapist's ability to think and rethink the patient plays a crucial role in the patient's recovery. This ongoing reassessment allows the therapist to remain open to recognizing changes; changes that should be shared with the patient, as it can reinforce motivation and foster further therapeutic engagement.

Neutrality and Abstinence

There is a beautiful poem, often attributed to Jorge Luis Borges, named "Poema a un Amigo" (Poem to a Friend) that captures how a person can be there for others without being interventionist in their life, but instead by simply being present. This poem can help us understand the concepts of neutrality and abstinence in psychotherapy.

> I cannot give you solutions for all of life's problems,
> nor do I have answers for your doubts or fears,
> but I can listen to you and share it with you.
>
> I cannot change your past or your future.
> But when you need me, I will be by your side.
>
> I cannot prevent you from stumbling.
> I can only offer you my hand so you can hold on and not fall.
>
> Your joys, your triumphs, and your successes are not mine.
> But I sincerely enjoy seeing you happy.
>
> I do not judge the decisions you make in life.
> I simply support you, encourage you, and help you if you ask me.
>
> I cannot set limits for you within which you must act,
> but I offer you the necessary space to grow.
> (Cultura Brillante. "Poema a un Amigo." Accessed 5 June 2024)

Nancy McWilliams (2011) discusses neutrality and abstinence as fundamental aspects of the psychoanalytic stance, exploring how these principles apply to contemporary practice and the therapeutic relationship. These concepts help define the therapist's role by establishing clear boundaries. A skilled therapist is emotionally invested in their patient's life, but like the poem, the strength of the relationship comes from being present in a particular way, not from directing the patient's life or assuming a position of authority or knowledge. This means keeping the focus entirely on the patient, avoiding alignment in the patient's internal conflicts, maintaining appropriate professional boundaries, and with a welcoming attitude.

The principles of neutrality and abstinence originated with Sigmund Freud (1912), who emphasized the therapist's role as a neutral mirror for the patient's projections and advocated for abstaining from gratifying the patient's desires to facilitate psychological work. Anna Freud (1936) further developed these ideas, stressing the importance of maintaining the therapeutic frame. Melanie Klein (1946) expanded on this by integrating active interpretation within a neutral framework, arguing that withholding gratification allowed patients to project their frustrations onto the therapist, thus shaping a more reserved therapeutic stance.

Supportive therapy, however, aligns more closely with the approach of Donald Winnicott (1953, 1960), who emphasized a flexible and responsive engagement with patients, highlighting the therapist's role in providing a holding environment. Similarly, Heinz Kohut (1971, 1977) prioritized empathic responsiveness over rigid abstinence, challenging the idea of the therapist maintaining a detached, "poker face" demeanour. Instead, both Winnicott and Kohut viewed the therapeutic relationship as one that fosters an environment where patients can feel held and understood, instead of a neutral mirror that can receive projections.

As we have seen, it is important to avoid fostering negative transference and prioritize ensuring the patient feels supported and protected within the therapeutic space. Supportive therapy avoids making the patient feel constantly frustrated with a therapist, for example, where the therapist won't answer simple questions about themselves. Unlike classic psychodynamic therapy, which refrains from gratification to focus on interpreting negative transference, supportive therapy recognizes that some patients may be too fragile to tolerate this approach and thus, it minimizes it as much as possible. It instead looks to build an alliance where the patient feels better after coming to see their therapist, not worse. If neutrality and abstinence are getting in the way, then the therapist needs to be flexible in a mindful way that will not turn the relationship into a friendship but will be more tolerable for the patient.

Neutrality does not mean emotional detachment, nor does it mean avoiding reassurance or encouragement. Instead, it requires a delicate balance, remaining close to the patient without colluding with their perspective. If a therapist aligns too closely with a patient's view, they risk reinforcing a dynamic in which the patient sees themselves as entirely right while others are wrong. This would not be therapeutic but rather a form of collusion.

For example, consider a case in which a psychologist told a patient that her difficulties stemmed from childhood trauma and placed sole blame on her mother. The patient already had a tendency to divide the world into victims (herself) and aggressors (everyone else). She struggled to take responsibility for her role in conflicts and found it difficult to acknowledge any good in others, including her mother, who, by all accounts, had done her best under challenging circumstances. While the psychologist may have developed a strong rapport with the patient, this came at the cost of further distancing her from her mother, reinforcing her pathological view of the world (this point will be explored further in the section *The Problem of Collusion*).

Validation involves recognizing and affirming the patient's emotions and efforts, helping them feel understood and supported, but not necessarily agreeing with their view. Rather than simply agreeing with the patient's narrative, the therapist acknowledges their experience in a way that is gentler and not colluding. For example:

- T: "Perhaps you are struggling to see all the hard work you have done."
- T: "Maybe there is a difficulty in giving yourself credit for what you have accomplished."
- T: "It sounds quite hard to have such a difficult relationship and feel that no one cares."

These statements communicate understanding while not requiring taking a side in a polarized argument. Crucially, validation must be genuine and in the moment, rather than relying on prefabricated phrases of encouragement.

Abstinence refers to the therapist's capacity to regulate their emotions and refrain from personal disclosure. However, abstinence does not mean being cold or distant. The therapist should remain a friendly and approachable presence while ensuring that the patient can use them in a meaningful way within therapy. Occasionally, minimal self-disclosure may be appropriate, but it must be carefully managed to avoid shifting the focus away from the patient.

For instance, a patient who struggled with feelings of abandonment due to an upcoming break once asked me, "Are you going back to Spain?" Recognizing his desire for connection, I simply replied, "Yes, I am." He followed up, "Where are you going, if you don't mind me asking?" I responded, "Asturias." This brief exchange broke abstinence, but in this context, it helped maintain a sense of connection before the break. The patient felt acknowledged rather than rejected.

However, at other times, it is important to maintain the therapeutic frame by not answering personal questions. The same patient later asked if I was a father. This time, I responded in a neutral but engaging way: "Today you are curious about me." He laughed, and the session continued. In this instance, we were not approaching a break, and the setting felt safer to gently deflect his question. Additionally, given the patient's tendency to treat me as a friend, it was important to reinforce professional boundaries.

In contrast, when a patient in psychodynamic psychotherapy asked if I was a father, I responded with an interpretation: "Perhaps you are wondering if I will be able to understand you." The patient reflected on this, acknowledging that he sometimes doubted whether people without children could fully grasp the challenges of parenthood. This response encouraged deeper exploration of his concerns rather than shifting the focus onto me. Similarly, when patients in psychodynamic psychotherapy ask about my background or holiday plans, I refrain from answering and instead consider what their curiosity might signify. While this can sometimes frustrate the patient or evoke feelings of rejection, such emotions are valuable within the psychodynamic process, as they open deeper material for exploration.

Ultimately, therapists must strike a complex balance: ensuring that the patient does not perceive them as a friend while also minimizing feelings of rejection or frustration. Supportive therapy emphasizes a sense of containment and reassurance, whereas psychodynamic psychotherapy invites patients to engage with more challenging emotions, including frustration with the therapist's non-disclosure. The key is to maintain a therapeutic stance that fosters trust, allows emotional engagement, and reinforces the professional frame.

Free Association

Free association is the counterpart to attentive listening, and both are key roles that the therapist and patient need to assume. These roles create a clear distinction between the two of them. The therapist facilitates free association by providing the space for it to occur. Initially, the patient may find this uncomfortable, and it is the therapist's role to help guide the process. Failing to establish this routine from the beginning can blur the roles, as it might lead to the patient taking control of the therapy.

Patients are encouraged to talk freely, without planning or imposing any agenda. This unfettered exploration, as Freud (1912) described in Recommendations to Physicians Practising Psycho-Analysis, involves the patient expressing thoughts that may be consciously avoided or deemed irrelevant. The therapist's role is to listen without judgement, maintaining open and unbiased attention, a practice Freud called "suspended attention." The therapist ensures that the patient feels safe enough to express anything without fear of being judged.

Free association allows the patient to shape the therapy according to their own needs, ones that are usually unconscious. This approach distinguishes supportive therapy from brief and other supportive interventions, as it focuses on mutual discovery rather than imposing early conceptualizations of the problem or setting predefined goals. The approach respects the patient's creative potential, which can often be their most effective tool in overcoming challenges.

In brief and goal-oriented work, the tendency is to overlook how important it is for the patient to feel listened to and supported, even if no immediate problem-solving takes place or specific goals are not achieved. While patients may begin therapy with a specific issue, such as grief, the process often leads to the discovery of their initial conflict. For instance, a patient of mine initially sought therapy for grief related to her sister's death. Over time, through free association and without a rigid direction, she began to explore an unresolved issue related to her mother's depression before and after her sister's death. By allowing the patient to follow these emerging themes, the therapist supports the patient in feeling understood. The patient is given space to listen to themselves, reflect, and reconstruct their own story at their own pace and when they are ready.

The therapist's role in this process is to listen carefully, clarify when necessary, and use other techniques that will be discussed later (Chap. 6). This helps the patient feel heard and ultimately supported. In supportive therapy, if the patient does not wish to explore a sensitive issue like bereavement and instead prefers to talk about something less charged, such as work, that is encouraged. At times, the therapist might gently encourage the patient to explore why a particular topic feels difficult, but there is no rush. If the patient feels the space is valuable and beneficial, it is perfectly acceptable for them to focus on work or other life aspects. The therapeutic space is about what is offered, not necessarily what is said, what matters is that the patient is listened to with care.

An example of this can be seen with a patient in a homeless service who was a chronic non-engager. One of my supervisees managed to work with her by giving her space to speak solely about her fish. While it may have seemed surreal, given the patient's serious, life-threatening problems, this approach proved effective. By engaging with the patient in this simple, non-threatening way, the supervisee managed to build a connection, helping her attend sessions and providing a crucial relationship during what were clearly very difficult times.

This is in contrast to more structured approaches that prioritize problem formulation and treatment planning from the outset. Such methods can lead patients to feel as though they are in a "paint-by-numbers" process, where the therapist imposes their expertise, techniques, or theoretical framework. This can limit the patient's opportunity to discover and share their own thoughts and emotions or simply have a space where they can talk without needing to adjust to someone else's ideals.

References

Abend, S. M. (1999). Chapter 1: The Problem of Therapeutic Alliance. *The Therapeutic Alliance, 73*, 1–16.

Adler, G. (1999). Chapter 5: The Alliance and the More Disturbed Patient. *The Therapeutic Alliance, 73*, 75–91.

Allison, E., & Fonagy, P. (2016). When Is Truth Relevant? *The Psychoanalytic Quarterly.*

Bion, W. R. (1962). *Learning from Experience.* Heinemann.

Bion, W. R. (1965). *Transformations: Change from Learning to Growth.* Heinemann.

Bion, W. R. (1970). *Attention and Interpretation: A Scientific Approach to Insight in Psycho-Analysis and Groups.* Tavistock.

Brenner, C. (1979). Working Alliance, Therapeutic Alliance, and Transference. *Journal of the American Psychoanalytic Association, 27*(Suppl), 137–157.

Caligor, E., Kernberg, O. F., Clarkin, J. F., & Yeomans, F. E. (2018). *Psychodynamic Therapy for Personality Pathology.* American Psychiatric Pub.

Carrere, R. A. (2008). Reflections on Psychoanalysis Conducted as a Talking Cure. *Contemporary Psychoanalysis, 44*(3), 400–418. https://doi.org/10.1080/00107530.2008.10745965

Carsky, M. (2013). Supportive Psychoanalytic Therapy for Personality Disorders. *Psychotherapy, 50*(3), 443–448. https://doi.org/10.1037/a0032156

Escandon, R. S. (2023). A Reflection on Self-Disclosure. *British Journal of Psychotherapy, 39*, 765–780.

Freud, S. (1912). Recommendations to Physicians Practising Psycho-Analysis. *The Standard Edition of the Complete Psychological Works of Sigmund Freud, 12*, 109–120.

Freud, S. (1923). The Ego and the Id. *The Standard Edition of the Complete Psychological Works of Sigmund Freud, 19*, 1–66.

Freud, A. (1936). *The Ego and the Mechanisms of Defence.* Hogarth Press.

Freud, S. (1937). Analysis Terminable and Interminable. *The Standard Edition of the Complete Psychological Works of Sigmund Freud, 23*, 209–254.

Goldberger, M. (2008). Discussion of "The Working Alliance and the Transference Neurosis" By Ralph R. Greenson. *Psychoanalytic Quarterly, 77*, 121–138.

Green, A. (2002). *Time in Psychoanalysis: Some Contradictory Aspects.* Free Association Books.

Greenson, R. R. (1965). The Working Alliance and the Transference Neurosis. *Psychoanalytic Quarterly, 34*, 155–181.
Hass, M., & Ardell, A. (2020). *Supporting Student Mental Health: Essentials for Teachers*. W. W. Norton & Company.
Hellerstein, D. J., Pinsker, H., Rosenthal, R. N., et al. (1994). Supportive Therapy as the Treatment Model of Choice. *Journal of Psychotherapy Practice and Research, 3*(4), 300–306.
Holmes, J. (2016). Psychotherapy Integration. Attachment: New Directions in Relational. *Psychoanalysis and Psychotherapy, 10*, 185–198.
Kernberg, O. F. (2003). The Management of Affect Storms in the Psychoanalytic Psychotherapy of Borderline Patients. *Journal of the American Psychoanalytic Association, 51*, 517–544.
Klein, M. (1946). Notes on Some Schizoid Mechanisms. *International Journal of Psychoanalysis, 27*, 99–110.
Kohut, H. (1971). *The Analysis of the Self: A Systematic Approach to the Psychoanalytic Treatment of Narcissistic Personality Disorders*. International Universities Press.
Kohut, H. (1977). *The Restoration of the Self*. International Universities Press.
Lemma, A. (2016). *Introduction to the Practice of Psychoanalytic Psychotherapy* (2nd ed.). Wiley-Blackwell.
Luborsky, L. (1984). *Principles of Psychoanalytic Psychotherapy: A Manual for Supportive-Expressive Treatment*. Basic Books.
McWilliams, N. (2011). *Psychoanalytic Diagnosis: Understanding Personality Structure in the Clinical Process*. Guilford Press.
Meissner, W. W. (2000). On Analytic Listening. *Psychoanalytic Quarterly, 69*, 317–367.
Novalis, P. N., Rojcewicz, S. J., & Peele, R. (1993). *Clinical Manual of Supportive Psychotherapy*. American Psychiatric Press.
Ogden, T. H. (2016). *Reclaiming Unlived Life: Experiences in Psychoanalysis* (1st ed.). Routledge.
Perez, G. O. (1996). Sobre la interpretación y el funcionamiento psíquico. *Revista de Psicoanálisis (APM), 23*, 65–77.
Pinsker, H. (1997). *A Primer of Supportive Psychotherapy*. The Analytic Press.
Sapisochin, G. (2019). Enactment: Listening to psychic gestures. *International Journal of Psychoanalysis, 100*, 877–897.
Shapiro, F., Kaslow, F. W., & Maxfield, L. (2007). *Handbook of EMDR and Family Therapy Processes*. John Wiley & Sons.
Sparer, E. A. (2024). The Psychoanalytic Situation: Frame and/or Setting. *International Journal of Psychoanalysis, 105*, 210–215.
Taylor, D. (2015). Treatment Manuals and the Advancement of Psychoanalytic Knowledge: The Treatment Manual of the Tavistock Adult Depression Study. *The International Journal of Psycho-Analysis, 96*(3), 845–875. https://doi.org/10.1111/1745-8315.12360

Temperley, J. (1984). Settings for Psychotherapy. *British Journal of Psychotherapy, 1*(2), 101–111.
Van der Kolk, B. (2015). *The Body Keeps the Score: Brain, Mind, and Body in the Healing of Trauma*. Penguin Books.
Werman, D. S. (1984). *The Practice of Supportive Psychotherapy*. Brunner/Mazel.
Wilson, M. (2018). The Analyst as Listening-Accompanist: Desire in Bion and Lacan. *Psychoanalytic Quarterly, 87*, 237–264.
Winnicott, D. W. (1949). Hate in the Counter-Transference. *International Journal of Psychoanalysis, 30*, 69–74.
Winnicott, D. W. (1953). Transitional Objects and Transitional Phenomena. *The International Journal of Psycho-Analysis, 34*, 89–97.
Winnicott, D. W. (1955). Metapsychological and Clinical Aspects of Regression Within the Psycho-Analytical Set-Up. *International Journal of Psychoanalysis, 36*, 16–26.
Winnicott, D. W. (1960). The Theory of the Parent-Infant Relationship. *The International Journal of Psycho-Analysis, 41*, 585–595.
Winnicott, D. W. (1965). *The Maturational Processes and the Facilitating Environment: Studies in the Theory of Emotional Development*. Hogarth Press.
Zetzel, E. R. (1956). Current Concepts of Transference. *The International Journal of Psycho-Analysis, 37*, 369–375.

CHAPTER 5

Beginning of Treatment

Beginning of Treatment

During the initial stages of a therapeutic relationship, the therapist should keep in mind that the primary function of supportive therapy is to maintain a stable, predictable, and ongoing therapeutic relationship as a consistent source of support. As will be discussed in the section on endings, interruptions in treatment are common, especially for patients with personality disorders who are nearly three times as likely to terminate treatment early (Cooper et al., 2004). Therefore, the therapist's initial task is to establish a secure-enough relationship and then actively maintain that relationship in a positive manner.

The key question is: How can the therapist foster a good relationship?

In supportive therapy, what the therapist avoids doing is just as important as what they actively do. Trying to be overly helpful or being consumed by anxiety about being "good enough" can push the patient away. An overly active therapist, who takes an approach that leaves the patient feeling confused or ignored, can also be counterproductive. It is crucial to avoid a domineering role, ensuring the patient has the space to navigate their own process. Practically speaking, the therapist should not interrupt the patient's narrative, keep their own interventions brief, allow the patient to direct the session, and, as previously noted, listen in an actively engaged way. In my experience shadowing sessions while working with

R. S. Escandon, *Contemporary Developments in Supportive Therapy*, Palgrave Texts in Counselling and Psychotherapy,
https://doi.org/10.1007/978-3-031-96059-8_5

homelessness, I observed that new supervisees, often feeling the pressure to prove themselves, would sometimes become anxious and talk excessively. They'd over-explain their methods, justify their actions, or try too hard to be liked, which often gave off a sense of desperation.

In addition to listening, the therapist can actively build mutual trust by demonstrating reliability, warmth, and empathy to foster a sense of collaboration. They should recognize the patient's needs and emotional state and adjust their approach accordingly, rather than imposing an agenda. Providing containment is essential, offering a stable and structured environment where the patient feels held, particularly in moments of distress. It is also important to respect the patient's pace, avoiding premature interventions that could overwhelm or alienate them. Showing some flexibility, such as being understanding about re-scheduling and fees, reinforces a sense of respect (Jacobs, 1999).

Another crucial factor is professionalism; not necessarily just in appearance, such as clothing or the aesthetic of the consulting office, but in the therapist's competence and preparedness. The therapist should convey an image of someone who has "been there, done that" and is therefore capable of handling the therapeutic space confidently. For example, a mistake I made when I saw my first patient in England, was failing to plan how I would receive payment. In the moment I improvised, jotting my details down on paper, which in hindsight, was not the level of professionalism I wanted to portray. The point here is that small moments of unpreparedness can make it harder for the patient to engage. Similarly, when a therapist changes consulting offices, refers a patient to an external agency for the first time, or needs to navigate NHS procedures, it's always best to prepare everything in advance. Ultimately, patients who are looking for conflict will find it, but it is the therapist's responsibility to minimize early negative reactions. In my experience, many patients who seem to be searching for something "wrong" are often simply scared. It's crucial to reassure them that they are in competent and professional hands.

During the actual sessions, the therapist allows the patient to express themselves freely without guiding their narrative, which might be sufficient for the patient at that time. It may feel like the patient is repeating the same conflicts, and the therapist might feel the urge to intervene differently, but if the assessment was correct, then this can be a good place to be and a "good enough" approach.

For example, a very humorous female patient came to see me during an emotional crisis. Her long-term partner had cheated on her, and he didn't seem remorseful. She coped by turning her pain into jokes, minimizing the seriousness of her situation. She could only attend once a week due to financial and work commitments. While she didn't exhibit characteristics of a personality disorder, it was clear that she came from a family background that did not foster emotional awareness. She struggled to think about or explore her emotions, as she had been raised to undermine them. She simply wanted a space, though she wasn't entirely sure what she was seeking within it.

Instead of interpreting her jokes, exploring their symbolic meanings, or addressing the seductiveness in her approach, I focused on providing a consistent, reliable space where she could be funny. I assumed that, within her social network, expressing genuine emotions would be seen as something negative and weak, and it would be wrong for me to expect she suddenly would do this. Over time, she realized how hurt, confused, and afraid she was beneath her humorous facade. My role was to help her find a place where it was okay to not to be okay and to hold her sadness in a way her social circle could not.

For a long time, I simply smiled when she made jokes and avoided laughing, as I considered this collusion. It was important to signal that therapy was a serious matter. However, she did manage to make me laugh a couple of times, and that was also okay. The space we created together was important. It was clear that a lot was happening that we were not talking about, but all of this was considered secondary to the space she was discovering. This marks a positive start. While it may appear that little has occurred, in truth, a strong foundation for something significant had been laid.

Another important element in the beginning is setting the frame. It's very common for patients to test the agreed-upon contract, and it's important for both the therapist and patient to settle into a routine where the hour, date, and time are respected by both parties. It is important to intervene casually if the patient arrives late or wants to change what was agreed upon. A firm contract promotes a sense of security. Ultimately, the first step of supportive therapy concludes when a predictable and stable therapeutic alliance has been established.

Middle Part of the Treatment: Understanding and Expression

Using the metaphor of a playground, imagine arriving at a public park with an 18-month-old toddler. The playground has classic play structures with swings, slides, and a sandpit. You intend for the child to play and enjoy themselves, but when you set them down, they might cling to your leg, hesitant to explore, or they might show interest in something entirely different, like touching a puddle or chewing on a stick. In such a situation, you might try to direct them to the swings, imposing a way of playing that feels more familiar to you.

In supportive therapy, the aim is to ensure that the patient feels safe to engage in their own process, much like the child exploring the playground. The therapist's role is to remove obstacles that hinder the patient's ability to express themselves freely, such as the fear of being judged. This freedom allows the patient to engage in creative expression, free from the constraints of the superego, utilizing illusion, symbolism, and fantasy (Ogden, 1985; Adler, 1989).

The therapist should focus less on the content and more on creating a safe environment, even if the patient's past experiences make this challenging. Just as we want the toddler to feel free to explore the playground at their own pace, the therapist must address the patient's negative expectations, which might be influenced by past relationships. For example, I often find myself saying things like:

- *It seems like you're afraid I'll judge you.*
- *Maybe you feel like I don't care about what you're saying, and that's why it doesn't feel safe here?*
- *I know you've mentioned negative experiences with men before, and since I'm a man, that could be making this harder for you.*

The therapist needs to address these obstacles proactively to help the patient feel more comfortable. It's also important to clarify misunderstandings, ensuring they don't reinforce negative transference. For instance, a patient once implied that I had overcharged them. In psychodynamic therapy, such distortions are sometimes left to unfold as part of the transference, but in supportive therapy, they should be addressed quickly and concretely. I simply said, "There seems to be a misunderstanding. We had this many sessions, and I charged this amount. If you'd like to review the payment, we can do so." Addressing these misunderstandings prevents distress from lingering and obstacles being created.

If, after a few months, a secure, predictable therapeutic space is established, the patient will likely feel more comfortable and familiar with the process. As mentioned, most dropouts occur within the first three months (Cooper et al., 2004), so preventing early termination can be a success story. One of my supervisees worked with a patient who had suffered the tragic loss of his wife and daughter in a car accident. He attempted suicide, became a heroin addict, and was referred to our service when he became homeless. Rather than focusing on processing his trauma or addiction, they provided him with a stable, human connection, listening to updates about his paintings and what he thought about TV shows. This approach was incredibly valuable to the patient and the team, although the local authority, which focused on recovery targets, will pressure for a different outcome. This highlights the significance of supportive work when professionals understand its true impact, providing the patient with someone they can rely on consistently and with stability.

Winnicott (1953) described a "third part of human life" between the inner world and external reality, where experiences of play and self-soothing occur. This transitional space is essential in adulthood, fostering creativity in art, culture, and spirituality. It allows for the use of symbolism and illusion, enabling a distinction between what is real and what is imagined. The caregiver's role is crucial in providing a safe environment for this creative space to grow (Winnicott, 1942).

When a patient uses the therapeutic space to talk about TV shows or about their paintings, they may be engaging in a manner where, beyond the surface content, there is a lonely, broken individual slowly allowing themselves to be reached. This space can be understood as a way for them to let someone care for them. This is why, in supportive therapy, it's crucial to create a therapeutic space that mirrors a positive early environment. It also explains why it can be so challenging to work within NHS and local authority target-based approaches, which often overlook the importance of the relational, non-goal-driven aspects of therapy.

Sometimes, creative play can take unexpected forms, serving as a metaphor for the patient's capacity to use the therapeutic space. For example, if I had interpreted my patient's jokes as resistance, I would have interfered with her process. When the patient talked about TV shows, it wasn't just avoidance of his addiction or trauma; it was his way of reconnecting with another human being. What each patient needs from therapy is completely different, and the metaphor of the playground as a blank slate, where the therapist is open to discovering how the space is used, is crucial to create an observing and open attitude.

In my view, play, as I define it, helps counteract splitting, a defence mechanism where the internal world becomes polarized. Play offers the freedom for new elements to emerge in a patient's narrative. Patients who struggle with play often find themselves stuck in repetitive loops, unable to incorporate new elements into their story. The therapist's role is to tolerate this without pushing, maintaining the therapeutic alliance, and supporting the patient's process. In other words, while constantly making jokes or only talking about TV might seem defensive, it could also be the very defence that allows the work to take place in the first place.

Middle Part of the Treatment: Avoiding Repetition

In Beyond the Pleasure Principle (1920), Freud introduced the concept of the repetition compulsion, suggesting that individuals who have experienced trauma tend to unconsciously repeat it in an attempt to master unresolved trauma by reliving it in new relationships or actions. However, rather than leading to healing, this repetition often traps individuals in a cycle where the past distorts the present. For example, someone who experienced domestic violence as a child may unconsciously find themselves in violent relationships as an attempt to confront or overcome their early trauma.

Aisenstein (2020) describes repetition as a paradox, both feared and craved. A neglected child, for example, may unconsciously provoke rejection in relationships as a way to validate the belief that they are unworthy of love. This dynamic extends into therapy as well: as patients grow closer to their therapist, they bring with them not only their relational patterns and unconscious dynamics but also the tendency to repeat traumatic events with the therapist.

Sandler (1976) suggested that both patient and analyst attempt to impose an intrapsychic object relationship on each other. If the analyst is unaware of these enactments, they risk reinforcing the patient's unconscious conflicts rather than working with them. Recognizing these subtle countertransference enactments is critical for deepening understanding, rather than getting trapped in them.

Repetition compulsion isn't just about overt emotional reactions; it can also manifest in the therapist's habitual ways of listening, interpreting, or structuring sessions (Jacobs, 1999). For instance, a therapist might be more distracted with one patient than another or might unconsciously adopt a different level of warmth or engagement. Supportive therapy presents unique challenges in this regard. The therapist's role is not to analyse transference patterns, and directly addressing them can often be counterproductive. However, ignoring them can result in premature termination. In the chapter *Active and Passive Use of the Transference*, I will explore how therapists can interpretively intervene to prevent destructive repetitions and potential abandonment. For example, breaks require careful handling. The therapist must acknowledge and interpret the patient's feelings about the break without going into early dependency, but to prevent the patient from acting out feelings of abandonment. Similarly, endings must be managed with equal sensitivity.

It is essential for therapists to identify when they are caught in a repetition and to find ways to break the cycle. A case that illustrates this can be seen with a patient who discovered that their analyst's daughter was getting married, which sparked many fantasies. Unconsciously, the patient had related to the analyst as a paternal figure, and this event symbolized the loss of a fantasy: the possibility of the analyst becoming their father-in-law. Feeling rejected, the patient reacted by attacking the analyst in the next session, criticizing their religion and other personal aspects, hoping to provoke an emotional response.

Rather than engaging in the dynamic, the analyst responded simply: "I am not sure why you are trying to do this, but you will not succeed." Without further explanation, the patient understood that they would not succeed in being rejected, as they had repeatedly experienced with their own father. The emotional wound of an unavailable father, which the patient had experienced in their early life, had almost been repeated in the analytic relationship. This brought back a dynamic where the patient preferred to be the one who ruined the relationship, rather than confronting the reality that their father was simply unavailable.

This case highlights the complexity of supportive interventions and shows how suddenly things can change when an unconscious conflict is triggered and repeated in such a powerful way. Pragmatically, it is essential for the therapist to remain responsive in their speech and behaviour without becoming reactive. This means avoiding intense emotional responses, which could risk unconsciously repeating the patient's destructive patterns. In the case above, had the analyst responded with irritation or dismissed the patient, they would have reinforced the patient's expectation of rejection.

Middle Part of the Treatment: Strengthening Ego Functions

As has been repeatedly highlighted throughout this book, the primary task is to ensure that the patient feels heard and contained. When the therapist introduces alternatives to listening, it can create the illusion that they are doing more by offering solutions rather than sitting with the patient's despair. This can lead the therapist into the territory of suggestion or placebo, ultimately taking away the patient's space to be truly listened to. That said, there may be times when interventions are necessary, depending on the circumstances the patient finds themselves in. However, before implementing these interventions, the therapist must engage in honest self-reflection and ask themselves whether the desire to intervene stems from a need to avoid silence and discomfort, or if there is a genuine need for a more active approach.

The idea of strengthening ego functions has been around for a long time. In the late 1930s, Anna Freud (1936) focused on the defence mechanisms of the ego, a concept later expanded by Heinz Hartmann (1964), who suggested that working with the patient's ego functions is crucial in helping them adapt to their environment. This process involves mediating internal conflicts and allowing for more functional, adaptive responses to external challenges (Gray, 1994).

The core concept is that the ego functions as a mediator between internal and external reality. By understanding and working with the ego's defensive mechanisms, the therapist can help alleviate pain. Defences, while sometimes adaptive, help the individual manage anxiety and conflict, and the therapist can influence the patient's functioning to facilitate greater emotional integration and adaptive responses (Gray, 1994). In practice, this involves helping the patient develop a stronger capacity for reality testing, emotional regulation, and impulse control. The aim is not to achieve deep structural changes in personality; rather, the therapist works to support and strengthen the patient's existing coping mechanisms, helping them manage their current conflicts more effectively. The focus is on improving how they cope with their experiences, rather than on how they can learn and grow from each experience.

A simple way of achieving this is by recognizing, encouraging, and reinforcing adaptive behaviours. One patient in his late 50s struggled with alcohol use and had recently started using heroin and crack cocaine. When he felt bad about himself, he would get drunk, look at pictures of his deceased brother and parents, and self-harm. However, he eventually escalated to using heroin or crack, depending on what his dealer could offer. He was overweight and started having panic attacks when coming off these drugs, feeling as though his heart was failing. The staff the service and I, frequently called ambulances, and because the paramedics weren't sure whether it was a heart attack, they always arrived quickly. They would then get frustrated when it turned out to be a panic attack. This became problematic in many ways for the service and the patient.

He was seeing one addiction therapist, but due to the escalation, I began joining the sessions in a joint format. We noticed that sometimes, he could sense when he was about to become depressed, angry, or anxious. He described it as something in his chest. He would then drink, and things would escalate as described. However, at other times, he would seek out a drinking partner or a friend to get drunk with and didn't end up using hard drugs. At this point, the other therapist recognized that while this was not ideal, it was an improvement. She pointed out how he was feeling better and emphasized how important it was for everyone that he managed his emotional problems in a better way.

It was meaningful for this patient to know that we all cared and noticed these differences. Reassuring the patient was therapeutic and containing. The other therapist suggested that the patient keep a drinking diary to track how much he drank and work towards reducing consumption. The patient would come eager to talk with the therapist, but she would ask about the diary, something he clearly didn't care for. It was clear that the patient was not being honest with these records, but he treated them as a kind of gift for the main therapist, a passionate young woman working hard, whom he appreciated. The problem with pushing for this intervention was that it became convoluted. He started lying and feared disappointing her, and the therapy began missing key relational elements because the diary turned the sessions into something more akin to CBT. The therapist was missing how important the relationship had become for the patient, and the diary and other interventions were irrelevant to him. The patient found more value in the genuine connection and understanding from the therapist, which was a crucial element in his progress, rather than the structured tasks that were introduced.

Positive reinforcement strengthens the patient's confidence and encourages them to continue engaging in adaptive behaviours. This can be done without the need for behavioural tasks that might alter the dynamic, creating a situation where the patient feels criticized, overwhelmed, or uncomfortable when they do work. A patient in supportive therapy has a sense that these interventions are for them and feel helpful. In contrast, I used to refer patients to a substance misuse service that would stop seeing patients if after a few months their diary didn't show a decrease in consumption. This approach shows how the focus can shift from the patient's emotional experience to the progress the therapist feels they need to see.

Patients in supportive therapy often experience fluctuations in their emotional state, and the therapist's role is to provide reassurance without allowing these crises to derail progress. The diary exercise, in particular, risks making the patient feel like a failure if they are unable to keep up with the task. The reality is that harm minimization, such as not using hard drugs, was an incredible result for this patient, who had been an alcoholic his entire life. Pushing for more progress was counterproductive. The therapist, motivated by the anxiety of the patient potentially dying (as multiple warnings had been received from the GP about his heart), wanted to change his habits and ultimately save him. An experienced psychotherapist, however, would stay with the patient's emotions, allowing the process to unfold without rushing or forcing change, and avoid creating a situation where the therapy breaks down.

When the patient experiences a setback, the therapist can act as a stabilizing presence. This may involve validating the patient's emotional pain while also reminding them of their capacity to cope and offering caring support. However, if the patient believes that their setback disappoints the therapist, it becomes problematic. The patient I am referring to stopped attending when he was drinking too much, because he felt we would be a disappointment. The first interaction of pragmatically encouraging a less harmful addiction was a success, but the second one completely changed the process.

In Chap. 6, I will provide a list and description of other similar interventions.

Endings

The process of ending therapeutic work is complex and multifaceted, involving numerous potential outcomes that both the patient and therapist must navigate together. In a safe therapeutic space, the topic of ending, or the decision to continue, should be explored multiple times throughout the process. At times, it may emerge as resistance to the work; at other times, it reflects a genuine reflection on the length and purpose of the process. However, the therapist should not shy away from discussing endings, even early in the process. Addressing the potential early ending prevents the patient from acting out their emotions by abruptly leaving, and in many ways, it should be embraced as a healthy part of the work.

Authors such as Ferenczi (1955), Balint (1950), and Bass (2009) have noted the difficulty in achieving a successful termination, with only a small proportion of cases reaching what is considered a proper ending. Glover (1955) also mentions how endings often occur for external reasons or due to symptomatic improvements, with patients leaving therapy prematurely rather than reaching a natural conclusion.

Something to consider is that endings and separations are experienced throughout the therapeutic process, whether triggered by the patient's personal experiences of loss or by interruptions like breaks and cancellations. When these moments are adequately managed, the conversation about the ending flows more naturally. Conversely, if a patient tends to miss sessions after a break or arrives late due to feelings of abandonment, and then pretend nothing emotionally meaningful is happening, it's likely that the topic of ending will arise in a similar way.

Endings in psychoanalysis are shaped by the interplay of perceptions of timelessness and the recognition of limits, requiring careful management by both patient and therapist (Bass, 2009). Time, in this context, is experienced subjectively, often complicating the process of termination, as a feeling of support, for example, can be unconsciously perceived as infinite or enduring. As if reliability is linked with everlasting.

A successful termination prepares the patient to move on, despite the inherent challenges and emotional strains of ending therapy. As mentioned previously, it may be necessary for a patient to begin analytic work or another intervention, but as time progresses, particularly in supportive therapy, it is important to question whether therapy is still serving the patient's needs or if it has outlived its usefulness. This reflection often marks the beginning of the ending conversation.

Ultimately, the end of therapy represents a developmental achievement, where patients fully take ownership of their experiences and assume responsibility for the conclusion of the therapeutic relationship, ideally in mutual agreement. The reason why this book focuses so heavily on avoiding early termination is that, while successful terminations are relatively rare, abrupt endings are quite common. A study conducted at the Columbia University Center for Psychoanalytic Training and Research reviewed all control cases from 1995 to 2000. Out of 163 patients who started psychoanalysis as control cases, nearly one-third (48 patients) terminated treatment prematurely. Over half of these early terminations occurred within the first six months (Cooper et al., 2004).

The reason early termination should be avoided is that patients often leave with a set of unchallenged fantasies. It is common for an early ending to trigger unconscious associations, such as the idea that affection or reliability should be endless. This can lead patients to feel rejected and create associations like "not being good enough," "damaging the relationship," or "making the therapist want to get rid of them," among others. The ending process should focus on ensuring that these fantasies are challenged, providing the patient with the opportunity to keep the good elements of the experience alive.

The easier part of endings in supportive therapy is that there are no specific goals to reach. The right time for an ending is simply when the patient no longer needs the space. This should be reflected on and reviewed, but the therapist doesn't necessarily need to wait for the patient to bring it up. If there are many sessions of silence or other clues, the therapist can invite the patient to consider the purpose of therapy. Similarly, if the therapist notices signs such as the patient arriving late or missing sessions, they can bring up the possibility of ending. An agreed ending that leaves the door open for the patient to contact the therapist again and concludes on a positive note, is more important than trying to keep the therapy going, especially if it results in an abrupt departure.

For example, a patient of mine had a traumatic birth. We worked together for 20 months, making significant progress regarding the initial distress of becoming a mother again. When it became clear that there was no longer a purpose for the sessions, I invited her to reflect on this. She was five months pregnant again and didn't want to end therapy until after giving birth, to ensure everything went well this time. We agreed on a tentative end date, six sessions after her delivery, and continued working until then.

Articulating out loud why she needed the therapy to continue was incredibly useful, allowing us to understand what was happening and ensuring the support was in place for a good ending. I believe she was conflicted and unsure of the purpose of the sessions, yet fearful of losing the space and potentially experiencing something difficult again.

Endings are often marked by ambivalence and loss, while at the same time, the way the end unfolds frames the entire process; much like how a good relationship, when it ends poorly, can be remembered negatively. It is an emotional time that both the patient and therapist struggle with.

From the patient's perspective, many factors can influence their reaction to the ending. These include their ability to accept their achievements, tolerate separation, their history of abandonment, and their tendencies towards idealization or devaluation. From the therapist's perspective, problems can arise if they fail to recognize that the ending involves ambivalence and loss for both the patient and them. Failing to recognize the impact of the ending can lead to enactments, one of the most common being the avoidance of addressing the ending until it is reached. This may result in the patient leaving abruptly or the therapist accusing the patient of an incomplete process, suggesting they need more therapy, which only leaves the patient feeling unsuccessful.

At the end of therapy, a significant change occurs as the relationship shifts from a pair to two individuals. This requires a process of bereavement of the therapeutic couple. During this time, ongoing understanding emerges about what has happened, what has changed, what remains unchanged, and which aspects of one's character endure. This period is marked by the simultaneous pain of mourning the work, the other person, the process, and oneself, while also finding joy in the experience (Jones, 2013).

Good-Enough Ending

There are no perfect endings in therapy, but a "good-enough" ending is characterized by three key elements.

First, the therapeutic pair must have discussed the ending and reached an agreement. It is important to ensure that the patient can cope without therapy and that the ending is not the result of unresolved conflict, such as the patient feeling unheard. If there is any lingering tension or disappointment, time should be given to address these feelings as much as possible. Hellerstein et al. (1994), Novalis et al. (1993), and Pinsker (1997) emphasize the importance of preparing for termination, processing the emotional responses associated with it, and ensuring a smooth transition for the patient into a relationship that will no longer be there. In a way means recognizing, it is not business as usual, and something is changing.

Second, fantasies about the ending should be recognized and challenged. There is a distinction between a patient who holds these suspicions but is open to questioning them and one whose fantasies have remained unexamined. For example, a patient once searched for information about me and discovered that I offer other kinds of therapy. He then developed the idea that I was ending therapy with him because he was not "smart enough" for more advanced work. This belief clearly resonated with his childhood experiences rather than our actual therapeutic process. In such cases, the therapist must address these fantasies directly and not allow the patient to leave therapy believing a false narrative. Since it is the end of therapy, the therapist can be more relaxed about abstinence. For example, I have told patients, "I really enjoyed working together," or "You seem convinced that I will be relieved not to work with you anymore, but that may not be the case—I might actually miss our work together."

By contrast, I once supervised a tutee who had agreed on an ending with a patient but avoided discussing it further. The patient, who had a long history of feeling inadequate and engaging in self-deprecating behaviours, stopped attending sessions and began self-harming. It was a challenging case, and it would be unfair to blame the therapist entirely, many things could have contributed to this outcome. However, the patient was left feeling "not good enough," and the therapist lost the opportunity to address this perception. The therapist genuinely enjoyed working with the patient, and it might have been beneficial to disclose this. The patient might have questioned it or felt sceptical, but at least they would have been presented with an alternative view.

Finally, the patient should feel that it is safe to return or contact the therapist, if needed. This demonstrates that the therapist remains a positive figure in the patient's life and that the therapeutic relationship ended on a reassuring note.

In NHS services and charities with a predetermined time frame, endings can be more challenging. The duration of therapy is agreed upon from the beginning, but the main difficulty arises when the therapy ends at a time that may feel premature, such as when the patient is feeling worse or when the therapy is just beginning to feel supportive. In such circumstances, the therapist must acknowledge the limitations of the setting. This should not be done in a self-deprecating or apologetic way but rather as an honest recognition that the patient is not at fault for the therapy ending. Pointing out the constraints of the service can help mitigate feelings of rejection or failure. In these cases, addressing unconscious fantasies becomes even more important. Patients often feel that they opened and that the therapist "couldn't handle it," when the structure of the service imposed the limitation.

The Problem of Collusion

Collusion is a serious concern in supportive therapy. Consider this common scenario: a patient seeks to build a unique, almost exclusive relationship with the therapist by complaining about others and positioning the couple on the same side. This might involve criticizing the immaturity of a family member, the lack of professionalism of a manager, or even sharing a particular viewpoint on a contentious issue. From a psychodynamic perspective, the patient is engaging in a psychological manoeuvre where the "bad" elements of humanity are projected outward, while the therapeutic relationship becomes a sanctuary of unity and goodness. This is what we call a split, a defence mechanism that divides the world into "good" and "bad" to create a sense of safety and connection. It's a common dynamic, often seen in families and couples who bond under the banner of a shared enemy.

In supportive therapy, this presents a unique predicament. If the therapist does not address the split, the patient may feel reinforced in their belief that the world is unfairly divided into a hostile "out there" and a safe "here." This can prevent the patient from integrating their own negative aspects and recognizing their tendency to split. However, working through this dynamic is inherently stressful. It requires the patient to tolerate the idea that the therapist may not always be on their side or share their perspective. It also demands an acceptance that the world is not black and white and that negative elements exist within everyone, including the therapeutic relationship and themselves. While this kind of thinking is essential for emotional maturity, it is also deeply challenging.

What happens in the therapeutic relationship? Does the therapist collude with the patient, reinforcing the belief that they are on the same team? The answer is no, but neither does the therapist directly challenge this dynamic. Instead, the therapist uses their psychoanalytic understanding to recognize what is happening and why. For example, they might detect that the patient is feeling persecuted and needs to split the world into "good" and "bad" to feel safe. However, the therapist does not intervene or interpret this. They listen without challenging, and if needed, they can signal how emotionally difficult it can be to feel in a particular way. This does not always work, and in Chap. 7, there is a list of interventions that can help manoeuvre such complex situations.

The key idea is that colluding such as in the previous example, where a psychologist reinforces a patient's belief that their suffering is entirely due to childhood and their mother's role, is not only neglectful but ultimately unhelpful. While it may initially bring relief to have the therapist confirm this black-and-white view of reality, the effect is short-lived. As Freud (1924) suggested, even in psychosis, there remains a fragmentary awareness of reality, despite the patient's denial.

If the therapist allows themselves to be drawn into this split world, they risk losing credibility, as the patient will eventually sense the artificiality of this dynamic. Instead, the therapist must remain grounded, acknowledging the patient's distress while leaving space for a more nuanced understanding to emerge over time.

Losing the Role

There are three main reasons why a therapist might lose their role. First, the therapist may become caught up in a process of enactment or projective identification. Second, the risk to themselves or others may become too high, requiring the therapist to shift to a different professional role. Third, this often occurs in NHS settings, where bureaucratic tasks, such as reviews or questionnaires, must be incorporated into the work. It could also apply when supportive therapy is used in a non-NHS setting, such as addiction treatment, where a different approach may be necessary.

Holmes (2016) explores how most therapists today adopt an integrative approach. For example, even in NHS settings that follow a psychoanalytic or psychodynamic framework, questionnaires such as the CORE-10 are commonly used to measure patients' progress and emotional well-being. This integration of CBT-based assessments within a psychodynamic framework illustrates how different therapeutic models are often merged in practice.

Many therapeutic approaches prioritize the therapeutic relationship, drawing from psychodynamic principles. However, when employing supportive interventions, it is crucial not to mix approaches indiscriminately, as this can undermine the effectiveness of the chosen modality. Consistency and predictability in the therapist's behaviour are key. As we have seen with the patient who was asked to keep a drinking diary, or for example, if a patient is struggling with emotional pain and the therapist finds it difficult to tolerate, resorting to a strategy-based approach.

In some cases, for example if a patient is suicidal, the therapist may need to consult other practitioners and assess suicide risk within a protective framework. While this disrupts the setting, it is sometimes the only viable way forward, requiring adjustments to the session structure and the therapist's stance of neutrality.

Losing the analytic role can have significant consequences, as it disrupts the predictability of the therapist's position and can push the patient into a position of uncertainty. This shift can introduce new dynamics into the therapeutic relationship. At times, reframing the process and establishing a new therapeutic agreement becomes necessary. For example, I once worked with a patient for over a year when he experienced a breakdown that led to him being sectioned. Following this, I offered a revised therapeutic contract to reflect the new circumstances, including the need for psychiatric care. This transparent approach ensured the patient understood the changes and provided an opportunity for discussion, fostering a collaborative solution that accounted for their reality.

Open and transparent communication is essential. For instance, it is important to inform patients if the therapist has had contact with anyone about them outside of sessions, and they should feel free to ask any questions about it. Transparency about the reasons for contacting external professionals, such as concerns for the patient's well-being, is crucial. On some occasions, I have been contacted by social services and asked to provide an opinion regarding a patient's potential risk to their family. Whenever possible, I inform my patients beforehand and discuss it with them first, especially if I am the one initiating the contact. The key principle is that patients should never be blindsided, and any change to the setting and the role is addressed and not kept from the patient.

References

Adler, G. (1989). Transitional Phenomena, Projective Identification, and the Essential Ambiguity of the Psychoanalytic Situation. *Psychoanalytic Quarterly, 58*, 81–104.

Aisenstein, M. (2020). Repetition and the Compulsion to Repeat, a French Perspective. *International Journal of Psychoanalysis, 101*, 1203–1214.

Balint, M. (1950). On the Termination of Analysis. *The International Journal of Psycho-Analysis, 31*, 196–199.

Bass, A. (2009). "It Ain't Over 'til It's Over": Infinite Conversations, Imperfect Endings, and the Elusive Nature of Termination. *Psychoanalytic Dialogues, 19*, 744–759.

Cooper, E. M., Hamilton, M. S., Gangure, D., & Roose, S. P. (2004). Premature Termination from Psychoanalysis: An Investigation of Factors Contributing to Early Endings. *Journal of the American Psychoanalytic Association, 52*, 1233–1234.

Ferenczi, S. (1955). The Problem of the Termination of the Analysis. In *Final Contributions to the Problems and Methods of Psychoanalysis* (pp. 77–86). Brunner/Mazel. (Original work published 1927).

Freud, S. (1920). Beyond the Pleasure Principle. *The Standard Edition of the Complete Psychological Works of Sigmund Freud, 18*, 1–64.

Freud, S. (1924). The Dissolution of the Oedipus Complex. *The Standard Edition of the Complete Psychological Works of Sigmund Freud, 19*, 171–180.

Freud, A. (1936). *The Ego and the Mechanisms of Defence*. Hogarth Press.

Glover, E. (1955). *The Technique of Psychoanalysis*. International Universities Press.

Gray, P. (1994). *The Ego and Analysis of Defense*. Jason Aronson.

Hartmann, H. (1964). Concept Formation in Psychoanalysis. *Psychoanalytic Study of the Child, 19*, 11–47.

Hellerstein, D. J., Pinsker, H., Rosenthal, R. N., et al. (1994). Supportive Therapy as the Treatment Model of Choice. *Journal of Psychotherapy Practice and Research, 3*(4), 300–306.

Holmes, J. (2016). Psychotherapy Integration. Attachment: New Directions in Relational. *Psychoanalysis and Psychotherapy, 10*, 185–198.

Jacobs, T. (1999). Chapter 2: On Beginnings: The Concept of the Therapeutic Alliance and the Interplay of Transferences in the Opening Phase. *The Therapeutic Alliance, 73*, 17–33.

Jones, A. A. (2013). "Now We're Out of Time": Thoughts on Endings in Poetry and Psychoanalysis. *The American Imago, 70*, 607–632.

Novalis, P. N., Rojcewicz, S. J., & Peele, R. (1993). *Clinical Manual of Supportive Psychotherapy*. American Psychiatric Press.

Ogden, T. H. (1985). On Potential Space. *International Journal of Psychoanalysis, 66*, 129–141.

Pinsker, H. (1997). *A Primer of Supportive Psychotherapy.* The Analytic Press.
Sandler, J. (1976). Countertransference and Role-Responsiveness. *The International Journal of Psychoanalysis, 53*, 43–47.
Winnicott, D. W. (1942). Why Children Play. In *Collected Works: Volume 2* (pp. 167–170).
Winnicott, D. W. (1953). Transitional Objects and Transitional Phenomena. *The International Journal of Psycho-Analysis, 34*, 89–97.

CHAPTER 6

Interventions

Interventions

Patient dropout is common in supportive interventions when working with individuals facing complex challenges such as substance misuse, homelessness, psychosis, offending, personality disorders, and other severe difficulties. A naïve assumption often exists that simply providing a reflective space, or a listening ear, will be enough for patients to appreciate therapy, engage meaningfully, and remain in treatment for as long as needed. However, for patients who are rigid in their actions and thinking, therapists may require a broader set of techniques to sustain engagement and facilitate communication.

It is crucial to consider the impact these tools have on the patient's ability to think independently and creatively. The therapist should avoid creating a dynamic in which the patient views them as the sole source of knowledge and guidance, thereby diminishing their own agency. Additionally, therapists must reflect on their own motivations; are these interventions genuinely being used to support the patient, or are they employed to ease the therapist's discomfort?

The recommendation is to use these techniques not as rigid solutions but rather resources for moments when therapy is at risk of breaking down, when a patient begins to withdraw or considers leaving. Below is a list and description of various tools therapists can use to navigate these challenges.

R. S. Escandon, *Contemporary Developments in Supportive Therapy*, Palgrave Texts in Counselling and Psychotherapy,
https://doi.org/10.1007/978-3-031-96059-8_6

Clarification

Clarification initiates a process of self-observation for the patient, prompting the therapist to seek explanations for any ambiguous or unclear information the patient has consciously expressed. This process not only helps the patient articulate and achieve a clearer understanding of their thoughts and emotions (Caligor et al., 2018) but also allows the therapist to deepen their understanding of significant aspects of the patient's life.

For example, during a session, a patient discussed their parent's history of infidelity, stating that their mother "had nothing to do with it."

T: "What do you mean by 'nothing to do with it'?"

P: "Well ... she knew my dad was seeing other women, and she would confront him angrily when he was caught. But what I meant is that she didn't take any action. Actually, that's not accurate either. It's more like she pretended not to see what was happening. It was obvious to anyone paying attention, but not to her."

In responding, the patient not only clarified their statement but also began to make sense of their own perspective. Through this process, they started to recognize that their mother had, in fact, taken a passive role, an aspect of the situation they would continue to explore in greater depth.

In supportive therapy, when a patient becomes angry or threatens to leave, clarification can be an extremely useful tool. The therapist can encourage expansion on a particular element. Asking questions such as:

> I hear that you feel I don't care. Can you help me understand what makes you feel that way?
>
> Have there been specific moments where you've felt I wasn't caring?
>
> It sounds like something I've done or not done has made you feel this way. Can you tell me more about what that's been like for you?

The goal is to create opportunities for the patient to elaborate on a rigid or concrete perception, opening space for reflection.

Confrontation

Confrontation in therapy is a risky yet powerful tool, especially when it's not the therapist's usual approach. Patients tend to react in different ways. Confrontation involves pointing out contradictions or omissions in the patient's material. These inconsistencies often reflect aspects of the patient's experience that are preconscious, denied, or rationalized (Caligor et al., 2018). By highlighting these discrepancies, the therapist draws the patient's attention to something important.

For instance, during a session, a patient remarked, "This kind of thing happens all the time. It's just part of dating, you know? I don't really care; it's just the dating scene in London."

T:	"I find that a bit suspicious."
P:(in a defensive tone):	"Suspicious about what?"
T:	"About you not caring."
P:	"Oh! Well, you know what I mean. It sucks, but that's life, you know? Sometimes they cry, sometimes you … not that I cried, but I did feel a bit down …"

In this example, the confrontation highlighted something that clearly affected the patient. Their attempt to appear indifferent masked underlying hurt.

Confrontation is a delicate therapeutic tool that can either help shift a patient's perspective in a constructive way or lead to conflict, particularly with individuals who are resistant to differing viewpoints. Another example, with a more challenging patient, arose when they said during a session that they had "almost always been on time." However, this was clearly not the case, and their lateness was starting to become a problem.

T: "I don't think that's correct. You've often arrived late, and there have been a few occasions when you didn't attend at all."

This approach is risky, as it carries an implicit accusation. However, the therapist achieves the important goal of addressing an issue that needs attention. Therapist don't want to make the patient feel trapped, but it's important to make a clear point. A less direct approach could be:

T: "I see it a bit differently. You've often arrived late, and there have been a few times when you didn't attend at all. Maybe we can think together about what's been going on?"

This approach might be easier for the patient to hear, as it frames the observation as a point of view rather than a fact. While gentler, it is less confrontational, depending on the circumstances a patient might just dismiss it.

The key element in confrontation lies not just in the content of what's being said, but in the tone and the shift in how the therapist typically intervenes. It is about signalling that this is not business as usual; this is something important.

Mirroring

The key problem with mirroring arises when it is used too frequently, mechanically, or superficially. When employed in this way, it can create something false that should be avoided. However, when used thoughtfully, mirroring can be an effective tool, especially in difficult moments.

This technique is particularly useful when working with patients who have severe narcissistic traits, as they may struggle to tolerate disagreement (Spotnitz & Meadow, 1976). Mirroring can help steer a conversation away from difficult dynamics and avoid a negative transference that the alliance is not strong enough to tolerate.

In simple terms, mirroring involves the therapist repeating part of what the patient has just said, either as a statement or a question. This can communicate a form of agreement with the patient, aligning with their current emotional state (Margolis, 1986).

For example, Margolis (1986) illustrates this technique with the following exchange:

P: "I slept poorly last night and feel tired today."
T: "You look tired."
P: "I feel miserable." (p. 22)

Through mirroring, the therapist reflects the patient's verbal or emotional communication to reinforce sense of attunement, allowing the patient to continue their story and demonstrating that the therapist has heard.

Another instance that exemplifies how this approach can be utilized arose during a challenging session before a summer break. This occurred when a patient arrived for their session and immediately said:

P: "I spoke with my wife, and she said it's not a good idea for me to continue therapy, so I guess this is our last session."

This disclosure stirred strong emotions in both of us. I suspected the decision was influenced by my upcoming break, sensing the patient was leaving therapy because he felt abandoned. However, I knew he would likely reject such an interpretation. In response, I mirrored his statement:

T: "Your wife thinks it's not a good idea to continue?"
P: "Yes, she thinks it's too expensive and it's not the right time."
T: "Not the right time?"
P: "Yes, well, if we're going to separate, we need all the money we can save."
T: "Well, if you're going to separate, perhaps it's the right moment to get help."
P: "Mmm, I guess you can see it that way."

By mirroring his first two statements, I was able to pace the conversation, maintain a calmer tone, and introduce pauses, which helped shift the session to a more introspective level. This allowed me to step out of the dynamic the patient had initially set after his first difficult statement. However, this wasn't easy for me either. In many ways, mirroring was a more accessible tool than attempting to formulate a complex interpretation or use a more intricate technique, especially given the high stakes and limited time, as he was leaving after that session. It also clarifies what I meant by a "rigid"; he wasn't offering an idea or feeling we could explore together, but was instead presenting facts in a rigid, unyielding manner.

Reframing and Naming the Problem

Reframing involves offering a different perspective on the same information, aiming to rationalize or reinterpret the patient's experience. On the other hand, naming a problem entails the therapist identifying the underlying conflict and gently bringing it to the patient's attention, which can enhance their understanding and help them cope effectively (Crisp & Gabbard, 2022).

P: "I hate it when this happens in my life. I want to be with my friends, to go out, but suddenly, they aren't there for me. I get really frustrated when they do this. Why can't they include me in their plans? I told them I was going to be away for a conference, but it got cancelled. If they had let me know, I could have been there. Instead, I see them having fun on Instagram, and I feel awful."

T: "It sounds like you feel left out, even though you were the one who told them you weren't available."

P: "Well, when you put it like that, it sounds silly. But I still think they could have told me they were going out ..."

In the example above, two things happened: the conflict was reframed, and the feeling of being left out was identified.

Emotional Validation

Emotional validation is a crucial element of supportive therapy, particularly for patients with challenging backgrounds who often feel isolated and misunderstood. By recognizing and acknowledging their emotions, therapists can soothe the part of the patient that feels neglected, helping them connect more deeply with their emotional experiences rather than feeling dismissed or unheard.

According to Borgogno (2016), emotional validation can significantly contribute to personal growth and give meaning to a patient's life events. It involves affirming the patient's feelings, thoughts, and experiences, or normalizing them when appropriate, which reduces their sense of isolation and abnormality (Pinsker, 1997). For instance, when a patient described their difficult interactions with a demanding and irrational mother, a simple acknowledgement like "*That sounds quite difficult*" helped them recognize their right to have those feelings rather than feeling guilty for having them.

Closely related to emotional validation is *naming an affect,* a technique that helps patients articulate their internal emotional states. What may begin as vague feelings can become more comprehensible when given a name, facilitating deeper self-understanding and connection to it

(Freedman & Russell, 2003). Dahl (1978) further explores this idea, noting that patients are not always aware of their emotions or may be uncertain if the therapist perceives them or is open to feel what they express. By naming these emotions, such as simply stating, *"You seem angry,"* therapists encourage patients' awareness of their emotional states, potentially shifting their perspective.

It is important not to become overly reliant on this technique. Research suggests that while initially identifying the patient's affect is important, it is not sufficient to create a meaningful therapeutic interaction (Holmes, 2009). Over time, the patient may become accustomed to the therapist's responses, which can make the interaction feel superficial or inauthentic. A more genuine response, conveyed through subtle nonverbal and verbal cues such as facial expressions, tone of voice, and emphasis, cannot be replaced by mere repetition. Constantly validating a patient's feelings, such as repeatedly acknowledging their sadness, can become incongruent with the therapist's body language and overall demeanour, especially if, over time, the therapist no longer genuinely feels what they are saying. This inconsistency may trigger a reaction from the patient, potentially leading to feelings of inauthenticity or disengagement.

Universalizing

Universalizing is a therapeutic technique in which the therapist connects the patient's personal experience to a broader human context, offering perspective and reassurance. This approach helps patients feel less isolated in their struggles, fostering a sense of connection and hope.

For instance, when a patient is overwhelmed by grief after a loss, the therapist might say, *"Right now, it may seem like there's no light at the end of the tunnel, but many people who have experienced similar losses find that, with time, healing becomes possible."* This intervention does not diminish the patient's pain but rather situates it within a wider human experience, highlighting the possibility of recovery.

Similarly, in cases involving substance misuse or mood disorders, therapists often integrate their clinical knowledge with supportive interventions by discussing these conditions in a universal context. This approach helps patients recognize that their struggles are not singular or abnormal, but rather shared by many others. Normalizing their experiences in this way can alleviate feelings of shame and self-blame, making space for self-compassion and feeling less uncertain.

Interpretation

Interpretation is a complex subject that stands as both a transformative approach and a potential pitfall in supportive therapy, depending on its careful application. It represents a complex junction where theoretical understanding meets practical implementation, allowing therapists to formulate hypotheses about the patient's inner workings.

However, the multifaceted nature of interpretation poses challenges. It can evoke stress and anxiety, emotions we aim to mitigate in supportive therapy, but it can also offer relief and better understanding of what the patient is going through.

In the following chapter, interpretation will be explored as an active intervention aimed at preventing negative transference, restoring communication, and reducing the risk of acting out.

The Ego-Supportive Techniques and Mentalizing

As we have seen, the ego is the structure that helps a patient navigate challenging situations. This section explores how the therapist can engage with the patient's capacity to address conflict and collaborate to tackle complex problems. Defences play a crucial role in psychological stability, allowing individuals to manage distress and maintain a sense of continuity. In supportive therapy, the therapist does not aim to dismantle these defences but rather to work with them in a way that ensures stability while encouraging greater flexibility when necessary. Some defences, such as repression or rationalization, can be adaptive, providing containment and helping the patient navigate overwhelming emotions. However, when defences become maladaptive leading to impulsive actions or severe distortions in perception, gentle interventions may be needed to prevent negative consequences.

Linked to these defences is the characteristic of reinforcing reality testing, which helps patients distinguish between internal experiences and external reality (Langs, 1975). Patients who struggle with projection, for instance, may develop significant distortions in how they perceive others. The therapist's role is not to confront these distortions directly but to facilitate a process in which the patient can explore their own assumptions.

Techniques from Mentalization-Based Therapy (MBT) can be particularly effective in these cases. Mentalization is the ability to reflect on one's own thoughts and feelings as well as those of others, thoughts that often become compromised during intense emotional states, leading to impulsivity and rigid thinking (Fonagy & Target, 2002). When a patient, for example, feels dismissed by the therapist, rather than challenging their perception outright, the therapist might say:

> It sounds like you felt I wasn't paying attention when you were talking about your probation appointment. What did you imagine was going through my mind at that moment?

After the patient expresses their perspective, the therapist can offer clarification:

> It's interesting that you thought I was dismissing you because I didn't care. When I looked away, I was trying to recall what happened last time you missed an appointment. In a way, you were right, I was distracted, but I was still thinking about you and our work together. It seems like your first assumption was that I wasn't interested in what you had to say.

Similarly, dynamic interpersonal therapy (DIT) (Lemma et al., 2011) emphasizes recognizing shifts in emotional experience over time, helping patients develop a more reflective and flexible mindset. A patient who initially felt comfortable in therapy but later expresses dissatisfaction to the point of wanting to leave may benefit from the therapist drawing attention to this change:

> For several months, it seemed like you felt comfortable in our sessions, but now you feel dissatisfied to the point of wanting to leave. That's quite a contrast. I wonder how both of these experiences might be true at the same time?

The therapist could also consider the following ways of mentalizing when working with the patient, as outlined by Holmes (2009):

- Self-mentalizing—being aware of one's own feelings.
- Other mentalizing—awareness of what the other might be feeling.
- Self-with-other mentalizing—recognizing what one might be feeling towards another.
- Other-with-self mentalizing—understanding what the other's feelings towards oneself might be.

- Self-and-other mentalizing—being able to observe interactions between oneself and another from a neutral vantage point. (Holmes, 2009, p. 12)

Another effective strategy is encouraging a third-person perspective, which helps patients create emotional distance and engage their reflective capacities rather than reacting impulsively. The therapist might ask:

> If someone you cared about was feeling the way you do right now, what would you say to them?

This intervention externalizes the emotional experience, reducing its immediacy and helping the patient approach their feelings with greater curiosity rather than certainty.

Crisis Plan

A crisis plan is a structured document that guides the response to situations where a patient may pose a risk to themselves or others. It outlines clear steps for both the patient and the multidisciplinary team to follow when serious concerns arise. The goal is to ensure timely, coordinated, and effective intervention while prioritizing the safety of all involved. A well-developed crisis plan should be so clear and accessible that would allow any new staff member to quickly understand their role, as well as the roles of others, in managing the situation.

A comprehensive crisis plan typically includes:

- *Clear Description of the Risk.* Detailing potential concerns such as overdoses, psychotic episodes, manic episodes, or offending behaviour. The plan should specify when the last incident occurred and assess the likelihood of it happening again.

  For example, if a patient recently overdosed yet continues using substances at the same level, their risk remains substantial. Likewise, a patient with a past episode of stress-related psychosis episodes who is currently under considerable stress, the potential for another episode should is higher.
- *Triggers and Warning Signs.* Identifying early signs of distress that may indicate a crisis is developing.

For example, I worked with a bipolar patient who would start feeling depersonalized before an episode. Any comment about him "not being himself" was a clear trigger. More common triggers include bereavement, anniversaries of losses, or past events that have previously led to distress.
- *Strategies.* Outlining the steps the patient can take to mitigate the crisis, which may include therapy, medication, or different coping techniques. This section should also clearly define the roles of each multidisciplinary team member when responding to the crisis.
- *Emergency Procedures.* Establishing specific steps to take if immediate intervention is necessary, including contact numbers for crisis services and escalation protocols.

In some settings, crisis plans may be referred to as a "risk assessment" alongside a separate "support plan." Terminology and format may vary depending on the service and the professionals involved. However, the key is that it remains an active document that clearly specifies crisis management responsibilities for both the patient and all staff members.

A crisis plan should always be developed in collaboration with the patient. Also, all professionals involved, including therapists, support workers, psychiatrists, nurses, care coordinators, social workers, and crisis team members, should be aware of the plan.

Any specific actions, such as referrals or medication adjustments, should be clearly stated to ensure accountability; a common practice is using the SMART approach:

- *Specific.* Clearly outline what needs to be done and who is responsible.
- *Measurable.* Define how progress will be assessed (e.g. regular check-ins, symptom tracking).
- *Achievable.* Ensure that the strategies and actions are realistic for both the patient and staff.
- *Relevant.* Tailor the plan to the patient's needs, history, and current situation.
- *Time-bound.* Set deadlines for actions, follow-ups, and reassessments.

Using this structured approach helps ensure that the crisis plan is both practical and actionable, facilitating timely intervention and support.

This approach also ensures transparency with the patient regarding confidentiality. It is essential that patients understand what information must be shared with other teams, particularly in cases where there are legal or safeguarding concerns.

For example, I once worked with a patient who had a history of sexual offending and was classified as a high-risk MAPPA 2 (Multi-Agency Public Protection Arrangements) case. His probation conditions explicitly prohibited him from having any device with internet access. He was aware that if he disclosed possessing a smartphone during our sessions, I would be required to report it.

On one occasion, he mentioned playing Xbox. I simply asked, *"Does it connect to the internet?"* He responded, *"No, I know I can't have that. It's an old one."* Although he was visibly upset by the question, he also understood that I had a responsibility to follow the crisis plan. This expectation had been clearly outlined in our therapeutic agreement from the start, reinforcing that my role included safeguarding both him and the wider community.

References

Borgogno, F. (2016). Narcissism, Psychic Recognition, and Affective Validation: A Homage to the "later Rosenfeld". *International Forum of Psychoanalysis, 25*, 249–256.

Caligor, E., Kernberg, O. F., Clarkin, J. F., & Yeomans, F. E. (2018). *Psychodynamic Therapy for Personality Pathology*. American Psychiatric Pub.

Crisp, H., & Gabbard, G. O. (2022). *Gabbard's Textbook of Psychotherapeutic Treatments* (2nd ed.). American Psychiatric Association Publishing.

Dahl, H. (1978). A New Psychoanalytic Model of Motivation: Emotions as Appetites and Messages. *Psychoanalysis and Contemporary Thought, 1*, 373–408.

Fonagy, P., & Target, M. (2002). Early Intervention and the Development of Self-Regulation. *Psychoanalytic Inquiry, 22*(3), 307–335.

Freedman, N., & Russell, J. (2003). Symbolization of the Analytic Discourse. *Psychoanalysis and Contemporary Thought, 26*, 39–87.

Holmes, J. (2009). *Exploring in Security: Towards an Attachment-Informed Psychoanalytic Psychotherapy* (1st ed.). Routledge.

Langs, R. J. (1975). The Technique of Supportive Psychotherapy. *American Journal of Psychotherapy, 29*(1), 3–16.

Lemma, A., Target, M., & Fonagy, P. (2011). *Brief Dynamic Interpersonal Therapy*. OUP.

Margolis, B. D. (1986). Joining, Mirroring, Psychological Reflection: Terminology, Definitions, Theoretical Considerations. *Modern Psychoanalysis, 11*, 19–35.
Pinsker, H. (1997). *A Primer of Supportive Psychotherapy*. The Analytic Press.
Spotnitz, H., & Meadow, P. W. (1976). *Treatment of Narcissistic Neuroses*. Center for Modern Psychoanalytic Studies.

CHAPTER 7

Active and Passive Use of the Transference

Active and Passive Use of the Transference

Interpretation is a fundamental concept in psychoanalysis, yet its meaning and application vary widely across different schools of thought and even between authors from the same school. Rather than adhering to a singular definition, psychoanalysts engage with interpretation in ways that reflect their distinct theoretical perspectives, clinical settings, and understandings of the therapeutic process (Druck, 2019). This diversity creates challenges for comparative analyses, as the very term "interpretation" lacks a universally agreed-upon meaning.

David Tuckett (2008) has highlighted the difficulties this presents, demonstrating how even within the same psychoanalytic tradition, practitioners may not share a common language for discussing core concepts. Similarly, Tuckett et al. (2008) encountered significant obstacles in attempting to delineate clear distinctions between psychoanalytic schools, as their theoretical boundaries often blur upon closer examination. Research by Levine (2013a, b) and Schafer (1979) echoes these concerns, illustrating the complexities of defining psychoanalysis as a unified discipline.

In this chapter, I will outline how interpretation can function as a tool in supportive therapy and contrast this with its contemporary application in psychoanalysis, highlighting key differences in technique and purpose.

R. S. Escandon, *Contemporary Developments in Supportive Therapy*, Palgrave Texts in Counselling and Psychotherapy,
https://doi.org/10.1007/978-3-031-96059-8_7

In supportive therapy, transference should be understood in a passive way, where the therapist is not actively focused on joint exploration, but instead uses their interpretation of the transference to understand and guide their practice. At the same time, when communication has become stagnated, there is potential harm or a clear evolution of negative transference, the therapist can use interpretation to help prevent a negative outcome.

Definition

Interpretation in psychoanalysis can be defined as the process through which the analyst makes unconscious material accessible to the patient, facilitating insight and emotional transformation. Freud (1900, 1913) initially conceptualized interpretation as a method of decoding symptoms, dreams, and resistances, likening it to a form of translation from unconscious to conscious thought. Over time, his technique evolved to emphasize transference interpretation, where the patient's relational patterns with the analyst reveal deeper unconscious conflicts (Freud, 1914).

Since then, many authors and schools of thought have contributed to the discussion, developing their own approaches to interpretation. However, this evolution has not followed a linear trajectory where each new development represents progress over the last. Psychoanalysis evolves in a complex and often fragmented manner, with theories not necessarily built upon one another and sometimes even contradicting each other. What we find in the history of interpretation is that each author has made particular use of this technique, tailoring it to their own theoretical understanding and the way they work.

This diversity in interpretative approaches underscores the challenge of defining interpretation as a singular technique (Tuckett, 2008; Levine, 2013a; Schafer, 1979). In clinical practice, interpretation varies across theoretical orientations, ranging from a classical emphasis on insight (Freud, 1913) to a contemporary focus on meaning-making within the therapeutic encounter (Hinshelwood, 1991; Caldwell & Joyce, 2014; Ferro, 2013, among many others).

In my view, good interpretative work in contemporary psychoanalysis is not like translation or a predefined intervention that can be switched on and off (like the tools reflected in the previous chapter). It is more of an attitude, an approach towards therapy, rather than a mechanical technique.

Consider this: for Freud (1915), the unconscious is made of imagery, lacking logic, linear time, and structured or secondary-process thinking. It is not something that we can directly perceive, but something we infer through dreams, lapses, symptom formation, free association, jokes, transference, countertransference, and so on. Therefore, if the therapist believes the task is to assign a fixed meaning to a particular word, action, or sentence, suddenly the unconscious has become a rigid and definable, losing the characterize already described, consider this analogy: imagine a painter sitting on the top of a mountain, trying to capture the landscape. Their work is not a direct translation of what they see, but an artistic interpretation, shaped by the conditions of that day like the light, the weather, and their own mood. It is not an exact description of the landscape, yet at the same time, it is not entirely divorced from the actual scene. It is an attempt to capture or sketch a characteristic of what the patient is perceiving in the moment, though this perception may shift by the next day. The aim is not to uncover an absolute truth, but to grasp something that feels particularly pressing or emotionally charged.

Antonino Ferro (2013) builds on Bionian and post-Bionian thought, suggesting that the analytic process is a form of co-narration, where patient and analyst co-create meaning. Ferro (2019) goes further by exploring the role of the analyst's imagination in the therapeutic process. He theorizes that the analyst's mind actively engages in transforming the patient's communications, treating them as dreams to be constructed in real-time within the analytic encounter.

Interpretation, then, is just not one thing that is said, but an ongoing work of exploration that can't be reduced to the last sentence the therapist gives to the patient. Just like a landscape can be defined by one painting.

For example, when a patient brings a dream. After exploring their associations and thoughts, I might offer a hypothesis or interpretation. The patient may reject it outright, but in doing so, they begin to think in a new direction and the session continues in a fluid movement, where the goal is not agreement or disagreement but to spark something that will lead to a co-creation of meaning.

The narrative that emerges in the session is not an objective truth, but a meaning that holds relevance for that moment. Just like a landscape painting, it might look entirely different the next day if the conditions change. Psychoanalysis is useful because the amalgamation of these experiences starts giving a different understanding to the patient, like how meta-analysis works in social science research. It is not the analysis of one result or one study, but instead, multiple studies come together to give a clearer picture.

Interpretation in supportive therapy, however, is a different matter, supportive therapy doesn't offer this kind of setting to the patient. Interpretation functions not as an ongoing stance but as a targeted tool, one that helps prevent harmful acting out, re-engages the patient when they are at risk of leaving the process, or facilitates reconnection in moments of rupture.

The goal is to show the patient a potential meaning underneath an action, or conscious thought, with the purpose of preventing something negative. For example, the patient may be scared and wanting to leave because something triggered a negative experience in the session, the therapist offers an observation that is giving an interpretation to the patient's situation. In what might be considered a little overly reductive, interpretation will look like:

> Perhaps, you see me as if I was your father/mother/ex....

In a way, this form of interpretation is a bit more classic, where the patient is being told that A = B: "Your feelings toward your therapist today = a previous experience with your father." There is no artistry in this; it is more akin to translation. Like Freud's (1922) interpretation of Medusa, where "*To decapitate = to castrate. The terror of Medusa is thus a terror of castration that is linked to the sight of something ... a boy, who has hitherto been unwilling to believe the threat of castration, catches sight of the female genitals*" (p. 273).

This way of interpreting is problematic. As Bollas (2018) noted, an excessive preoccupation with transference interpretation can develop in the therapist's mind, leading to a rigid and overdetermined approach. It also reinforces the cliché of "you mean me" interpretations (Budd & Rusbridger, 2005), where the therapist pushes every piece of material the patient brings into a framework that seeks associations or parallels with the therapist, ultimately offering those links to the patient.

As mentioned before, in supportive therapy however, the therapist's use of interpretation is primarily to intervene in ways that prevent the escalation of negative transference, restore communication, or help the patient avoid acting out. As such, interpretation should not be used excessively or routinely, nor should it necessarily be centred on transference. Finally, the attitude of the therapist offering support cannot be the same as that of a psychoanalyst offering psychoanalysis. The therapist is not aiming for a cooperative, explorative approach. Instead, the attitude should reflect a focus on reducing anxiety and providing support.

Prevent Escalation of the Negative Transference

One of the reasons negative transference is avoided in complex cases is that challenges arise when a patient is unable to question their projections, perceiving the therapist as embodying a negative figure from their past. Hanna Segal (1998) described this inability to reflect on or question such projections as a lack of symbolic formation, where there is no subjective position. The core idea is that before the patient reaches a crisis point, the therapist can intervene while the patient is still more receptive, flexible, and willing to engage.

Key moments in therapy that often trigger these dynamics are the therapist's breaks. Separation is a complex emotional process that, in early life, can lead to attachment difficulties since it can evoke fears of abandonment and feelings of rejection in the patient. In supportive therapy, a helpful approach is to prepare the patient for such circumstances. However, patients are often unaware of how difficult the break will be for them, leaving the therapist with the task of interpreting and anticipating their emotional response.

The way this unfolds in practice varies, as the therapist typically uses material the patient brings into the session to introduce the theme of separation. For example, after informing the patient about an upcoming break, the therapist might notice the patient expressing dissatisfaction with seemingly unrelated experiences. The patient might complain about how they were treated in a restaurant, then go on to criticize how people nowadays only care about money. The therapist might interpret this as an indirect expression of how they feel about the therapy; that perhaps they fear the therapist only cares about money.

While the interpretation may not be entirely accurate, its purpose is to spark curiosity in the patient about their own feelings regarding the upcoming break. Rather than approaching separation as an intellectual concept, this approach invites the patient to explore their already-existing emotional experience.

The aim is to help the patient process their feelings before the break occurs, reducing the likelihood that they will act out their unexamined emotions, such as by leaving treatment abruptly because they feel abandoned themselves.

Restore Communication

After a break, patients may struggle to feel comfortable and may distance themselves from the therapy. As Quinodoz (2003) points out, some individuals defend against the fear of separation by denying emotional needs or clinging to an illusion of self-sufficiency. Returning to therapy may challenge this belief, causing them to withdraw further or even attempt to leave the process to assert their independence.

Quinodoz (2003) suggests that therapists work towards restoring communication with these patients by acknowledging their underlying fears of dependency and loss. He advises against confronting the patient directly about their avoidance, as this may heighten resistance. Instead, the therapist should gently explore how the patient's fear of dependency shapes their behaviour, emphasizing the therapist's steady and containing presence to help the patient face separation without feeling abandoned. I would also suggest highlighting that their withdrawal might stem from the process being consistent and meaningful to them, leading to a fear of losing it. Emphasizing the positive aspects of the process can help the patient feel more secure and valued within the therapeutic work.

When verbal communication is difficult, Quinodoz (2003) recommends using metaphors, dream interpretation, and symbolic language to help patients express their feelings. He observes that breaks in communication often reflect transference dynamics, where the patient may perceive the therapist as rejecting or abandoning them. Interpreting these dynamics at the right moment can help the patient re-engage in therapy. As Luborsky (1996) suggests, the function of interpretation in these cases is to link transference dynamics with the patient's associations, enabling self-reflection and therapeutic change, particularly in moving away from negative transference.

Avoiding Acting-Out

The therapist should observe and form hypotheses based on the transference, and allow these insights to inform their work, but not necessarily act on them by means of interpretation. This passive approach to interpretation is the hallmark of supportive therapy, where only when a patient is about to act out, the therapist can use interpretation to hold the patient. The aim is to minimize the negative impact their behaviour may have on their life, helping the patient reflect on the dynamics at play and offering a different perspective that can guide their actions in a more constructive direction.

For example, a patient who had significant financial needs, was about to lose her job because she kept clashing with her manager during her probation period. It was clear that the manager was trying to resolve things, but the patient seemed intent on portraying him as an abuser and herself as the victim. This is where the therapist may have a dynamic hypothesis about the patient's behaviour that could help. In this case, it was evident that the patient's unresolved early conflicts had been projected onto the manager. She envied her father to such an extent that she struggled to speak with him and hadn't seen him in years. She saw him as a wealthy man who left her in poverty, and she couldn't tolerate her envy towards her parents' wealth. When she spoke about her manager, she would use similar expressions, as if suggesting he "had it all." My interpretation here aimed to help her avoid being fired and losing a job she needed. The goal was to offer her a different perspective on the dynamic she had been trapped in. This usually comes with a challenge because the patient felt I was blaming her when I suggested thinking about the situation in relation to her past experience. However, it did spark some reconsiderations.

References

Bollas, C. (2018). *The Freudian Moment*. Routledge.

Budd, S., & Rusbridger, R. (Eds.). (2005). *Introducing Psychoanalysis: Essential Themes and Topics*. Routledge.

Caldwell, L., & Joyce, A. (2014). Essentially Winnicott: Creating Psychic Health. *British Journal of Psychotherapy, 30*, 18–32.

Druck, A. B. (2019). Freud's Papers on Technique and Contemporary Clinical Practice: By Lawrence Friedman. *International Journal of Psychoanalysis, 100*, 631–634.

Ferro, A. (2013). The Meaning and Use of Metaphor in Analytic Field Theory (with G. Civitarese). *Psychoanalytic Inquiry, 33*, 190–209.

Ferro, A. (2019). *Psychoanalysis and Dreams*. Routledge.

Freud, S. (1900). The Interpretation of Dreams. *The Standard Edition of the Complete Psychological Works of Sigmund Freud, 4*, ix–627.

Freud, S. (1913). Totem and Taboo: Some Points of Agreement Between the Mental Lives of Savages and Neurotics. *The Standard Edition of the Complete Psychological Works of Sigmund Freud, 13*, vii–162.

Freud, S. (1914). On Narcissism: An Introduction. *The Standard Edition of the Complete Psychological Works of Sigmund Freud, 14*, 67–102.

Freud, S. (1915). The Unconscious. *The Standard Edition of the Complete Psychological Works of Sigmund Freud, 14*, 159–215.
Freud, S. (1922). Medusa's Head. *The Standard Edition of the Complete Psychological Works of Sigmund Freud, 18*, 273–274.
Hinshelwood, R. D. (1991). Psychodynamic Formulation in Assessment for Psychotherapy. *British Journal of Psychotherapy, 8*, 166–174.
Levine, H. B. (2013a). *Unrepresented States and the Construction of Meaning*. Karnac.
Levine, H. B. (2013b). Comparing Field Theories. *Psychoanalytic Dialogues, 23*, 667–673.
Luborsky, L. (1996). Theories of Cure in Psychoanalytic Psychotherapies and the Evidence for Them. *Psychoanalytic Inquiry, 16*, 257–264.
Quinodoz, J.-M. (2003). *The Taming of Solitude*. Routledge.
Schafer, R. (1979). On Becoming a Psychoanalyst of One Persuasion or Another. *Contemporary Psychoanalysis, 15*, 345–360.
Segal, H. (1998). 'The Importance of Symbol-Formation in the Development of the Ego' — in Context. *Journal of Child Psychotherapy, 24*, 349–357.
Tuckett, D. (2008). *Psychoanalysis Comparable and Incomparable*. Routledge.
Tuckett, D., Basile, R., Birksted-Breen, D., Böhm, T., Denis, P., Ferro, A., Hinz, H., Jemstedt, A., Mariotti, P., & Schubert, J. (2008). Illustrations. *Psychoanalysis Comparable and Incomparable: The Evolution of a Method to Describe and Compare Psychoanalytic Approaches, 61*, xi.

CHAPTER 8

Intercultural Aspect of Supportive Therapy

Intercultural Aspects of Supportive Therapy

This chapter examines the crucial role of dependency in human development, highlighting how our survival relies on social connections from birth. It explores how early brain development is geared towards social interaction and language, essential for survival and identity formation. This leads to the internalization of cultural norms and societal influences, shedding light on how our sense of self and relationships are shaped by social context, ultimately creating an intercultural phenomenon that becomes an active ideological component of the therapeutic dynamic.

Human Dependency and Social Development

We can start with the fundamental idea that human survival as a species relies heavily on the support of others. From birth, humans depend on one another for assistance, from feeding and clothing to cleaning, protection, and meeting basic needs. Unlike other primates, humans are born relatively premature, lacking the strength, movement, and spatial awareness that many primates have from birth. In fact, humans would require an additional 14 months of gestation to develop the innate abilities that other primates possess at birth (McNamara, 2002). This early dependency on others for care drives infants to prioritize social interaction as a crucial

R. S. Escandon, *Contemporary Developments in Supportive Therapy*, Palgrave Texts in Counselling and Psychotherapy,
https://doi.org/10.1007/978-3-031-96059-8_8

tool for survival, linking their development closely to others and the social components of society.

From birth, human brain development focuses on what is known as the "social brain." Unlike many species, human cranial sutures stay open after birth, allowing for growth until puberty and fostering the development of connections in the neocortex, which governs social cognition and impulse control. Early on, humans prioritize social understanding, learning to interpret and manage interactions while regulating behaviour like aggression and sexuality through social engagement (Cozolino, 2014). Humans have a fundamental need to belong and feel connected to others. Foulkes (1948) highlights that throughout history, belonging to social groups has been essential for survival and adaptation, providing protection, resources, and opportunities for cooperation.

Language plays a crucial role not only in facilitating effective communication and interaction with others but also in shaping how we describe, understand, and express ourselves. Humans begin learning words before they can engage in complex thought, meaning language precedes much of the understanding that forms social awareness. At the same time, language inherently carries deep societal significance, where words and their meanings represent the undigested aspects of society within all of us (Harland, 1987).

This is not simply a matter of being born in France and speaking French; rather, words have the power to capture aspects of human experience, enabling a progressive discovery of oneself within a linguistic and cultural framework. Additionally, as Elias (1991) demonstrates, language is not just a collection of words but the means by which we can coordinate our experiences in relation to ourselves and others.

Beyond verbal communication, affection and social norms also function as a language. Whether a parent kisses their child on the lips or refrains from doing so is shaped by societal expectations, subtly imposing cultural boundaries on the child. Through gestures of love and care, a social and political world is transmitted, shaping the child's understanding of relationships and personal limits.

Laplanche's (2005) concept of enigmatic meaning highlights how unconscious parental desire influences identity within a cultural and social framework. When a mother kisses her baby in a socially acceptable way, she not only expresses affection but also transmits implicit cultural norms and unconscious meanings that the infant will later attempt to translate. These interactions embed the child in a structure of social expectations, where human subjectivity is shaped by both unconscious transmission and external norms. Society dictates what is deemed appropriate or inappropriate in expressions of intimacy, reinforcing how individuals experience relationships and their own sense of self.

The Human and Others

Freud (1914) explains that from the infant's perspective, there is no distinction between the external world and them. The infant experiences a state of undifferentiation, where the environment and the infant feel like one indivisible entity. Freud suggests that the infant initially believes the external world belongs to them, as part of their own being, only later to realize this is not the case. This process of recognizing an external world is fraught with challenges. Authors like Rosenfeld (1964) describe a primary narcissism, where, due to separation anxiety and their own destructiveness, the individual may deny the existence of anything that doesn't belong to them, thus avoiding the painful experience of separation. Steiner (1993) discusses how an individual may resist abandoning a state of omnipotence and control, where the distinction between self and other is not clear. As adults, these individuals may acknowledge a world beyond themselves and can physically differentiate between self and other, but they struggle to view the world independently of their own projections. Britton (1989) suggests that individuals can lack the ability to recognize an external reality beyond their subjective experience and find it difficult to perceive the world as independent from their own desires and perceptions.

We have two key components: an individual who is inseparable from society, absorbing its social messages from their caregiver, and using language to discover and define themselves, with the potential struggles to separate their own experience from their subjective understanding of the world. A third component is the incorporation of societal norms. As Freud (1921) suggests, as individuals grow older, they will no longer rely on their parents to reinforce these norms; instead, they will police themselves, aligning their behaviour with their own ideals result of oedipal identifications. With this foundation, we can begin exploring the intercultural aspects that are formed within the individual.

The Human and Culture

Multiculturalism, starting in the 1960s, suggested that prejudice stemmed from ignorance of each other's ways of life, and that familiarity would end prejudice. However, it overlooked unconscious mechanisms like projection (Dalal, 2015), where individuals take their own fears and place them onto others, assuming them to be a threat. This projection creates a dynamic where avoiding others becomes necessary, as the person unconsciously places their own unwanted traits onto them. Society creates stereotypes and social groups that separate them from others and at the same time give them a group identity. Tajfel (1981) argues that individuals derive a sense of self from the groups to which they belong, and group membership influences perceptions they would have of others. For Tajfel, social stereotypes emerge as a way to categorize people into in-groups (the groups we belong to) and out-groups (those we perceive as different). A creation of a split between society into an us and them.

These social stereotypes are part of broader social constructs formed through interaction, as individuals and groups create, interpret, and maintain shared meanings about the world (Berger & Luckmann, 1967). We do not experience external reality directly; rather, our perception of what is real is continuously shaped through language, communication, and social practices. As Gergen (1991) suggests, while an objective world may exist, our access to it is mediated through socially constructed narratives, making any claims about its true nature inherently interpretive.

Claude Lévi-Strauss (1976) compared social structures to a deck of cards, where though they may differ in colour and suit, they share the same fundamental numbers. Similarly, all societies, from aristocratic elites to Amazonian tribes, rely on regulatory systems to govern aspects like marriage and alliances, adhering to underlying patterns that define what is permissible or not.

For Freud (1924), the resolution of the Oedipus complex marks the point at which social norms are internalized. It is through adherence to these norms that identity is shaped. For example, if an individual identifies with their father, and in the future, only dates people of the opposite sex, like his father did with his mother, implicitly they are classified within the social group of heterosexuals. Freud explains:

> The object-cathexes are given up and replaced by identifications. The authority of the father or the parents is introjected into the ego, and there it

> forms the nucleus of the super-ego, which takes over the severity of the father and perpetuates his prohibition against incest, and so secures the ego from the return of the libidinal object-cathexis. (pp. 176–177)

The authority of the father, once internalized, dictates not only moral prohibitions but also expectations regarding sexuality, gender identity, monogamy, nationalism, religion, and social ambition. Through this process of identification with the parent of the same sex, the individual unconsciously adopts these norms, shaping their sense of self and replicating the patterns of those who came before them. However, as Roudinesco (2003) suggests, Freud's interpretation of the Oedipus myth reflected the social anxieties of early twentieth-century Vienna, particularly its deep-seated fear of the feminine and its fixation on sexual difference. She argues that Oedipus' transgressions symbolized an attack on paternal authority, generational hierarchy, and the family structure. As a result, the Oedipus complex was deployed as a political tool, ensuring that its "proper resolution" required women to accept their supposed castration, abandon autoerotic pleasure, and embrace heterosexual monogamy.

A similar critique was put forward by French philosophers Gilles Deleuze and Félix Guattari (1972), who viewed Freud's Oedipus complex as a mechanism for repressing desire and enforcing conformity in service of capitalist structures. However, this may not have been Freud's intention. Butler (1990) offers an alternative reading, emphasizing Freud's recognition that sexuality and gender are not biologically fixed but shaped by external influences and unconscious processes. She argues that with Freudian theory, gender is not something one *is* but something one *does*, a repeated performance of actions, gestures, and discourses that create the illusion of a fixed identity. In this sense, social norms are not natural but socially constructed and imposed upon individuals.

Foucault (2012) takes this further, arguing that what is considered "truth" or "knowledge" is produced through discourse and institutional power. These socially constructed beliefs shape how individuals understand themselves and the world, reinforcing normative structures through education, law, and cultural practices which are then internalized.

Norms that shape identity, particularly those related to sexuality, are products of social power structures. Incest is not inherently immoral but a taboo accepted in some societies and condemned in others. Symington (2004) argues that incest is wrong because one must symbolically "eliminate" the father, an idea Freud (1913) also proposed, portraying an authoritarian father who claims exclusive rights over "his" women and enforces laws against both incest and patricide to protect his power. However, this perspective applies primarily to monogamous societies. In cultures where polygamy is practised, rejecting the father is not necessary, highlighting that moral transgressions are defined by social norms rather than absolute ethical principles. Like incest, polygamy is merely another taboo, shaped by the prevailing social order.

Navigating the landscape of taboos and social constructs, Slavoj Žižek (1989) expands on this by understanding ideology as an unconscious structure that shapes our perception of reality. It operates at an unconscious level, influencing how people interpret their social world while remaining unaware of its effects. Ideology works by generating a fundamental illusion, one that individuals accept as reality. Unlike Foucault or Freud, who emphasize external imposition, Žižek argues that ideology is actively internalized. It has a subjective dimension, shaping how individuals relate to their desires and to others. People engage with ideology not just because it is enforced, but because it provides a framework through which they navigate their unconscious desires and fantasies about themselves and the world.

Intercultural in Psychotherapy

As we have seen, social constructs, ideology, stereotypes, rules, taboos, and prejudices are not just inevitable aspects of human experience but also fundamental to understanding our work. Likewise, they play a crucial role in how patients understand themselves. In this way, interculturalism manifests in three key ways in the consulting office:

1. The dynamic between patient and therapist, where differences in ethnicity, sexuality, social class, and any other category, brings into the couple the potential of social discourse. (The couple they form together, mixed race, for example.)
2. As a lens for understanding the patient, recognizing that therapy itself is shaped by subjective and cultural influences. Intercultural aspect will shape the therapist's hypothesis of their patient. (What the therapist brings)
3. Through the patient's lived experience, where their cultural background and personal history shape their identity and psychological processes. (What the patient brings)

The dynamic between patient and therapist inevitably leads to an "us versus them" mentality, shaped by differences in race, class, religion, and other social divisions. Social psychology shows that we unconsciously reinforce these categories, exaggerating similarities within groups and differences between them (Tajfel, 1981). It can create a sense of deep inability to relate by making it seem like we have more in common with people who look like us or identify similarly, and less with people who don't.

Race, for example, is a social construct—it has no real biological foundation—but it is deeply embedded in the unconscious, shaping an individual's internal world, identity, and relational dynamics (Mintchev, 2018). In the therapy room, if the therapist is white and the patient black, the therapist inevitably carries personal and cultural biases. Theories of whiteness examine how racial identity and privilege are constructed, shaping social power and subjective experience (Morgan, 2021, 2024). Whiteness is not just about white identity but about how societal structures normalize and privilege white perspectives, often marginalizing people of colour.

In connection with this, Fakhry Davids (2011) proposes that individuals internalize societal stereotypes and prejudices, leading to the development of an "internal racist structure" within the mind. This internalization positions the racial "Other" as an object in the mind, influencing how individuals perceive and interact with those they perceive as different, forming an internal prejudice that patient and therapist will have of one another.

By recognizing and confronting internalized prejudices, individuals can foster more equitable and empathetic interactions across social differences. This perspective is crucial in psychotherapy, as social conflicts, whether related to race, gender, immigration status, socioeconomic class, or sexual orientation, inevitably shape the therapeutic space and must be addressed. It is not enough to simply claim, "I am not racist" and leave it at that; deeper reflection is required. As Davids (2011) suggests, we all carry internalized prejudices, particularly against marginalized groups, which often serve as scapegoats in societal discourse.

However, prejudice is not solely the therapist's concern; patients from marginalized backgrounds may also internalize negative stereotypes about themselves and others. This highlights the broader impact of societal attitudes, not just in areas like race, gender, and sexual orientation but also in mental health. Stigma surrounding mental illness, homelessness, sex work, offending, and substance misuse significantly affects individuals' quality of life. Negative societal perceptions can lead to self-stigma, where individuals internalize these views, resulting in diminished self-esteem, social withdrawal, and poorer mental health outcomes.

Technique

There is no silver bullet for addressing such a complex topic, and I won't pretend to have one, especially when more and more books continue to emerge, attempting to grapple with this complexity. My invitation is to consider social phenomena as an inherent part of the therapeutic relationship, rather than reducing everything to transference, as if all difficulties stem from the patient's early childhood experiences which are then projected.

For example, I once worked with a gay patient who felt that I couldn't possibly understand what it meant for him to grow up in a small rural English town. I certainly couldn't know firsthand what it was like to be gay in that particular time and place that are too different to my personal experience. But I was never meant to know. A problem would have occurred if I dismissed his feelings by interpreting them solely as negative transference or a mistrust issue. Or if I had treated his experience as mere projection, when in fact, homophobia is a social reality that should not be reduced purely to an unconscious dynamic.

This is not about bringing politics into the consulting room and falling into the dichotomies of the broader culture war social discourse. Being liberal is as much a social construct as being racist; both are ideological positions, and the therapist's role is not to endorse any particular stance. Rather, it is about maintaining analytic thinking that can give an insight into the unconscious dynamic and an openness, being able to receive the patient's experience fully, while also recognizing that feelings of guilt, anger, shame, or accusation may arise in the process. These are not merely transference phenomena; they belong to the social world we inhabit.

A useful analogy can be drawn from the COVID-19 pandemic. Suddenly, patients became aware that their therapists were going through the same crisis as them. Both were affected by lockdowns, restrictions, and uncertainty. This created a different dynamic, one of shared experience. In contrast, if a patient struggles with relationship issues or work-related stress, they do not expect their therapist to share those specific conflicts. Similarly, psychosocial dilemmas exist within this shared dimension, where both therapist and patient participate. Both have been shaped by experiences of prejudice, having both suffered from and contributed to it.

Practically speaking, avoiding excessive caution is key. It is possible to speak clearly *and* make space to understand the patient's social reality. For instance, while working at the Tavistock with colleagues who have written extensively on these topics, I noticed how common it was for them to ask cultural questions directly. They might simply ask me, "Where are you originally from?" without the need for hesitant phrasing like "May I ask?" or "Do you mind if I ask?", as this might already imply there is an issue. It was clear that they asked because they noticed my accent and while I sometimes feel insecure about my accent, those feelings are mine to process. If their question feels difficult or painful, it is not because they asked, it is because I need to work through my own response to it. This direct approach opens a door for such conversation, but it would be harder if they feel they can't ask, or if they feel they have done something wrong. In this clear way, they touch on my prejudice, not theirs.

It is important to address this topic so that every aspect of the human condition can be spoken of in therapy. If a black patient has a white therapist who is afraid to talk about race, then the patient is left with an incomplete therapeutic work, one in which certain topics are rendered too dangerous to address. Instead, through care and openness to the other's experience, the therapist can initiate these conversations. They may get it wrong, and getting it wrong is part of the process of understanding each other's experiences. The key is not to become defensive, too fearful of saying the wrong thing, and to remain open-minded.

References

Berger, P. L., & Luckmann, T. (1967). *The Social Construction of Reality: A Treatise in the Sociology of Knowledge*. Open Road Media.

Britton, R. (1989). The Oedipus Complex Today: Clinical Implications. In R. Britton, M. Feldman, & E. O'Shaughnessy (Eds.), *The Oedipus Complex Today* (pp. 89–113). Karnac.

Butler, J. (1990). *Gender Trouble: Feminism and the Subversion of Identity*. Routledge.

Cozolino, L. (2014). *The Neuroscience of Human Relationships: Attachment and the Developing Social Brain* (2nd ed.). W.W. Norton & Company.

Dalal, F. (2015). Prejudice as Ideology: The Creation of "Us" and "Them" Groups in Society (and Psychoanalysis). *Psychotherapy and Politics International, 13*(3), 182–193.

Davids, M. F. (2011). *Internal Racism: A Psychoanalytic Approach to Race and Difference*. Palgrave Macmillan.
Deleuze, G., & Guattari, F. (1972). *Anti-Oedipus: Capitalism and Schizophrenia*. University of Minnesota Press.
Elias, N. (1991). *The Symbol Theory*. Sage.
Foucault, M. (2012). *The Archaeology of Knowledge*. Vintage. (Original work published 1969).
Foulkes, S. H. (1948). *Introduction to Group Analytic Psychotherapy*. William Heinemann Medical Books.
Freud, S. (1913). Totem and Taboo: Some Points of Agreement Between the Mental Lives of Savages and Neurotics. *The Standard Edition of the Complete Psychological Works of Sigmund Freud, 13*, vii–162.
Freud, S. (1914). On Narcissism: An Introduction. *The Standard Edition of the Complete Psychological Works of Sigmund Freud, 14*, 67–102.
Freud, S. (1921). Group Psychology and the Analysis of the Ego. *The Standard Edition of the Complete Psychological Works of Sigmund Freud, 18*, 65–144.
Freud, S. (1924). The Dissolution of the Oedipus Complex. *The Standard Edition of the Complete Psychological Works of Sigmund Freud, 19*, 171–180.
Gergen, K. J. (1991). *The Saturated Self: Dilemmas of Identity in Contemporary Life*. Basic Book.
Harland, R. (1987). *Superstructuralism*. Methuen.
Laplanche, J. (2005). *Essays on Otherness*. Routledge.
Lévi-Strauss, C. (1976). *El hombre desnudo [The Naked Man]*. Siglo Veintiuno Editoriales.
McNamara, K. J. (2002). Changing Times, Changing Places: Heterochrony and Heterotopy. *Paleobiology, 28*(4), 551–558.
Mintchev, N. (2018). Object-Relations and Cultural Narratives in the Analysis of Racism: Theorizing Subjectivity After Klein and Lacan. *Psychoanalytic Dialogues, 28*(2), 234–249.
Morgan, H. (2021). *The Work of Whiteness*. Routledge.
Morgan, H. (2024). The Work of Whiteness. *The Journal of Analytical Psychology, 69*, 758–767.
Rosenfeld, H. (1964). On the Psychopathology of Narcissism: A Clinical Approach. *The International Journal of Psycho-Analysis, 45*, 332–337.
Roudinesco, E. (2003). *La Familia en Desorden [Family in Disorder]*. Fondo de Cultura Económica.
Steiner, J. (1993). *Psychic Retreats: Pathological Organizations in Psychotic, Neurotic and Borderline Patients*. Routledge.
Symington, N. (2004). *The Blind Man Sees, Freud's Awakening and Other Essays*. Karnac.
Tajfel, H. (1981). Social Stereotypes and Social Groups. In J. C. Turner & H. Giles (Eds.), *Intergroup Behaviour* (pp. 144–167). Blackwell.
Žižek, S. (1989). *The Sublime Object of Ideology*. Verso.

Index

R. S. Escandon, *Contemporary Developments in Supportive Therapy*, Palgrave Texts in Counselling and Psychotherapy,
https://doi.org/10.1007/978-3-031-96059-8

The manufacturer's authorised representative in the EU is Springer Nature Customer Service Centre GmbH, Europaplatz 3, 69115 Heidelberg, Germany. If you have any concerns regarding our products, please contact ProductSafety@springernature.com

Printed and bound by CPI Group (UK) Ltd, Croydon, CR0 4YY
30/09/2026
02225576-0006